SONG-WRITING WITHOUT BOUNDARIES

SONG-WRITING WITHOUT BOUNDARIES

LYRIC WRITING EXERCISES FOR FINDING YOUR VOICE

PAT PATTISON

AUTHOR OF
WRITING BETTER LYRICS

Writer's Digest Books
An imprint of Penguin Random House LLC
penguinrandomhouse.com

Printed in the United States of America
22nd Printing

ISBN 978-1-59963-297-1

Edited by Scott Francis
Designed by Claudean Wheeler

ABOUT THE AUTHOR

Pat Pattison is a professor at Berklee College of Music, where he teaches lyric writing and poetry. His books *Writing Better Lyrics*, *The Essential Guide to Lyric Form and Structure*, and *The Essential Guide to Rhyming* are considered definitive in their genre and have earned many ecstatic reviews. In addition, Pat has developed four lyric writing courses for Berklee's online school, available through patpattison.com, and has written more than thirty articles for a variety of industry publications. His internationally successful students include multiple Grammy winners John Mayer and Gillian Welch. He continues to present songwriting clinics across the globe.

Pat's website is: http://patpattison.com.

THANK YOU

My deepest gratitude to the many writers who participated in these challenges. You've set a high bar, and your work will both instruct and inspire. You've marked out an enchanting path for writers to follow, and as they do these challenges, they surely will fall in love with your writing. I did.

To my many students. Your passion, curiosity, and creativity continue to embiggen me on a daily basis.

To the songwriters, artists, and industry professionals who participate in my annual student Spring Break Trip to Nashville. Your generosity over the last two and a half decades has transformed so many lives.

To my colleagues at Berklee College of Music. Your drive to find a stronger, clearer way to say it continues to enlighten me.

To Mike. You write a mean foreword, buddy.

To Jason, Suzanne, Maia, Olivia, and Holly, just for being you.

To my wife, Clare. You make everything better.

TABLE OF CONTENTS

Foreword by Mike Reid ix
Introduction 1

Challenge #1: Object Writing

DAYS 1-5: "What Writing" 10
DAYS 6-8: "Who Writing" 23
DAYS 9-11 "When Writing" 31
DAYS 12-14: "Where Writing" 39

Challenge #2: Metaphor

DAY 1: Adjective-Noun Collisions 51
DAY 2: Finding Nouns From Adjectives 59
DAY 3: Finding Adjectives From Nouns 63
DAY 4: Noun-Verb Collisions 67
DAY 5: Finding Verbs From Nouns 70
DAY 6: Finding Nouns From Verbs 74
DAY 7: Expressed Identity: Noun-Noun Collisions 77
DAY 8: Expressed Identity: Noun-Noun Collisions 81
DAY 9: Expressed Identity: Finding Nouns from Nouns 84
DAY 10: Playing in Keys: Using Linking Qualities 88
DAY 11: Playing in Keys: Using Linking Qualities 92
DAY 12: Playing in Keys: Finding Linking Qualities 93
DAY 13: Playing in Keys: Finding Linking Qualities 95
DAY 14: Simile 98

Challenge # 3 Object Writing With Metaphor

DAYS 1-3: Linking Qualities to Target Ideas 107

DAYS 4-7: Working Both Directions.. 122

DAYS 8-11: Finding Linking Qualities: Working One Direction 143

DAYS 12-14: Finding Linking Qualities: Moving Both Directions... 158

Challenge # 4: Writing in Rhythm & Rhyme

DAYS 1-2: Tetrameter Lines.. 175

DAYS 3-6: Tetrameter Couplets 179

DAYS 7-10: Common Meter 190

DAY 11: Tetrameter and Pentameter 201

DAYS 12-13: Common Meter and Pentameter................................ 205

DAY 14: Unstable Structure: abba 212

Afterword 224

FOREWORD

I don't like forewords, afterwords, prefaces, author's notes, or introductions in books. But Pat's been a friend for a long time and against all common sense, he asked me to do this. I could say no only so many times.

Not long ago I said to Pat, "Why bother with all this when great lyrics don't seem to matter anymore?" "They matter to you, don't they?" he shot back. And there it was. For reasons beyond my full understanding I had to confess that they did matter to me. A lot. If they matter to you, buy this book. It won't tell you what you should write about. Getting off the couch and out into your own life will do that. What it will do is teach you how to write. Best of all, it will teach you how to think like a writer.

Talent is a mystery, a gift, a discovery of oneself. Technique, on the other hand, is just plain hard work and for me, the single greatest challenge of writing well has always been in understanding what I mean to say. It's not what others think you should be saying, but what you and you alone mean to say.

How, then, do we break through the barriers of the well-ordered conscious mind and get to where the honest impulses, the richest ideas, the deepest passions live? Waiting on the muse to ascend is a fool's errand. If you're of a mind to want to get at the best in you, you hold in your hands, at this moment, a tool of inestimable value. Mark Twain said, "The difference between the right word and the almost right word is the difference between lightning and the lightning bug." Faithfully following the principles set down in this book will not only help you find the right word but, more importantly, will be a constant companion in the lifelong journey toward understanding precisely what it is you mean to say.

Over the years, Pat and I have disagreed more than a little on many things. But I take no issue with his deep, abiding desire to help those who choose to write, write better.

Mike Reid
Nashville, TN
July 2011

INTRODUCTION

For us, there is only the trying.
The rest is not our business.

—T.S. ELIOT (EAST COKER, FROM *THE FOUR QUARTETS)*

This is a book on writing. And it is a book *for* writing. For writers of all kinds: songwriters, poets, playwrights, novelists, bloggers; anyone who loves the taste of words. It challenges you to take a journey into yourself to discover not only what you have to say, but also to discover an authentic voice to say it with.

Finding your voice as a writer is a lot like finding your voice as a singer. If you can carry a tune, you can learn to do it better. You can find, by exploration, where your voice feels strongest, where it feels the most like you. You try different styles, different timbres, different approaches and, slowly for some, more quickly for others, the real you emerges. The feeling you get when you hit that bulls-eye is like no other feeling. You're incredibly alive and centered, like you've pushed your roots deep into the earth's core. But committing to a journey to find that unique voice takes work; it takes practice.

Even if you have massive talent, you can learn to do it better, and with more consistency. Great singers use vocal coaches. Even in their prime, they continue the search.

Writing is like that, too. You have a writing voice, something that feels the most like you. Your job is to find it.

This book will help you find your writing voice. It will help you do the work it takes. And, it will help you practice.

I got the idea for this book from observing how effectively 14-day challenges focused and improved my students' writing. 14 days is short enough to be manageable, but long enough that it stretches you, forces you to come up with ideas, *to just write about something*, rather than be paralyzed by needing to find that great idea. In my experience, great ideas are more likely to present themselves *while* you're writing than while you're not. The 14-day challenge took the fear out of my students' writing and put the fun back in. It can do that for you, too.

I decided to set four 14-day challenges to help you explore your writer's voice more fully. Each challenge asks you to concentrate on a different facet of your writer, to explore, not only how you *think*, but the stuff of your *senses*, then to relate those senses to the outer world, transforming them into metaphor.

The first 14-day challenge, Object Writing, asks you to respond to three prompts each day, of 10 minutes, 5 minutes, and 90 seconds. It will help you be more vivid and specific in your writing, and the timed writing will help your speed and efficiency.

The second challenge is on metaphor. It asks you to use your newfound skill at sense-bound writing in a step-by-step process for finding metaphors. By the time you finish, you should be a pro. This challenge also contains timed writing to help you chop away the underbrush in your writing faster.

Then challenge 3 asks you to extend metaphors, learn to explore them deeply, and see them from reversed directions: both "a pack of hungry wolves is a hurricane," and also "a hurricane is a pack of hungry wolves." You'll write a 5 or 10 minute response to each prompt, mostly four pieces each day.

The final challenge asks you to do it all in rhythm and rhyme. Again, because the writing is timed, it forces you to go deep, quick.

It teaches you to think ahead rhythmically and manipulate rhyme more fluidly.

If you do all these challenges, I suggest you take a short time between them to let the swelling subside a bit. I also strongly suggest that you find a friend or friends to do the challenges, someone to share your work with. That way, you're responsible to someone and they're responsible to you. You'll both have an audience and a cheerleader. It's pretty neat.

What I love about this book is what made it so much fun to write. Every prompt in the book has two sample responses from other writers. I asked a bunch of writers to jump into the challenges, and also set up an international Object Writing contest, using the prompts in the first challenge. I even had a few writing parties at my house.

Writers across the globe did these challenges and submitted their responses for possible inclusion in this book. As the responses came in, I got more and more excited. What fine examples they were! Fun to read. Instructive. On target. It was a joy to see so much creative, imaginative work. But winnowing so much amazing writing down to only two examples per prompt was torture.

I think you'll benefit from their examples as much as I did.

In my commentaries I've tried to focus your attention on some specific issue raised by a prompt or an example, but when other interesting issues or techniques come up, I respond to them, too. Your reading should be fun and instructive, at least I hope it is.

But the writing, that's what you're here for. The work. The practice. The writing.

CHALLENGE #1

OBJECT WRITING

★ ★ ★ ★ ★ ★ ★ ★ ★ ★ ★ ★ ★ ★ ★

Don't tell me the moon is shining;
show me the glint of light on broken glass.
—ANTON CHEKHOV

Turn down the lights, Turn down the bed
Turn down these voices inside my head.
"I Can't Make You Love Me" —**REID/SHAMBLIN**

Where do these words take you? Do they make you see something? What kind of bed? Single? Double? What color is the bedspread? The pillows? Where is the light coming from? A table lamp? Above the headboard?

When a lyric stimulates and provokes your senses, you draw the images from your own experiences. You fill Mike Reid's and Alan Shamblin's words with *your* stuff. They involve you, so the song becomes *about you*. That's the power of sense-bound writing. It pulls the listener into the song by using his own memories as the song's material.

I've got sunshine on a cloudy day
When it's cold outside, I've got the month of May
"My Girl" —**SMOKEY ROBINSON**

Sense-bound writing turns observers into participants. It is one of the most powerful tools a writer has.

> The sea is calm tonight.
> The tide is full, the moon lies fair
> Upon the straits; on the French coast the light
> Gleams and is gone; the cliffs of England stand;
> Glimmering and vast, out in the tranquil bay …
> "Dover Beach" **—MATTHEW ARNOLD**

The best way I know to exercise the sense-bound writing muscle is to use a technique called "object writing." Object writing is timed, sense-bound writing usually done first thing in the morning.

You pick an object—a real object, like a paper clip, a coffee cup, a Corvette—and treat it as a diving board to launch you inward to the vaults of your seven senses:

Sight Sound Taste Touch Smell Body Motion

Although you're familiar with five of your senses, you could probably stand a few exercises to sharpen them, especially the four you don't normally tap into when you write. If I asked you to describe the room you're in, your answer would be primarily, if not completely, visual. Even if it is only visual, remember that visual has at least three aspects—color, shape, and texture. Try isolating each and noticing, for example, only shapes. Look for similar shapes. Then look for texture "rhymes." How many colors does the tree really have?

Try spending a little time alone with each sense. How big does the room sound? (If it were twice as big? Half as big?) How would the table taste if you licked it? (No, it's not silly. You just lick more selectively because Mom warned you all about germs.) How would the rug feel if you rubbed your bare back on it? How does the kitchen table smell? Remember this, it is important: The more senses you incorporate into your writing, the better it breathes and dances. Take your time and practice.

The two additional senses need greater explanation.

1. *Organic sense* (body) is your awareness of inner bodily functions, for example, heartbeat, pulse, muscle tension, stomachaches, cramps, breathing. Athletes are most keenly focused on this sense, but you use it constantly, especially in responsive situations. I've been sitting here writing too long. I need a back rub.
2. *Kinesthetic sense* (motion) is, roughly, your sense of relation to the world around you. When you get seasick or drunk, the world around you blurs—like blurred vision. When the train you're on is standing still and the one next to it moves, your kinesthetic sense goes crazy. Children spin, roll down hills, or ride on tilt-a-whirls to stimulate this sense. Dancers and divers develop it most fully—they look onto a stage or down to the water and see spatial possibilities for their bodies. It makes me dizzy just thinking about it.

TIMED WRITING

It's important that you time your object writing. Make it a manageable task, one that you feel good about doing every day. And do it first thing in the morning.

Guarantee yourself only the time allotted for each prompt. Set a timer, and stop the second it goes off. I mean the *second,* as you'll see from some of the examples in this challenge. Be sure you always stop right at the buzzer. Don't finish the sentence. Don't even finish the word you're in the middle of. You're much more likely to sit down to a clearly limited commitment than if you get on a roll some morning and let yourself write for thirty minutes. Then, guess what you'll say the next morning:

1. "Ugh, I don't have the energy to do it this morning (remembering how much energy you spent yesterday), and besides,
2. I've already written enough for the next two days. I'll start again Thursday."

Breaking the timed commitment is how most people stop morning writing altogether. Any good coach will tell you that more is gained practicing a short time each day than doing it all at once. Living with it day by day keeps writing on your mind and in your muscles.

Two beings inhabit your body: you, who stumbles groggily to the coffeepot to start another day, and the writer in you, who could remain blissfully asleep and unaware for days, months, even years as you go about your business. If your writer is anything like mine, *lazy*, or even *slug*, is too kind a word. Always wake up your writer early so you can spend the day together. It's amazing the fun the two of you can have watching the world go by. Your writer will be active beside you, sniffing and tasting, snooping for metaphors. It's like writing all day without moving your fingers.

Soon, during your timed writing, something like this will happen: Your writing will start to roll, diving, plunging, heading directly for the soft pink and blue glow below when, beep! The timer goes off. Just stop. Wherever you are. Stop. Writus interruptus. All day your frustrated writer will grumble, "Boy, what I might have said if you hadn't stopped me." Guaranteed, when you sit down the next morning, you will dive deeper faster. You'll reach the bottom in three minutes flat. Next time, one minute. Finally, instantly. That is your goal: immediate access—speed and depth. So much information and experience tumbles by every minute of your life, the faster you can explore each bit, the faster you can sample the next. But, of course, speed doesn't count without depth. The ten-minute absolute limit is the key to building both. And it guarantees a manageable task. Look:

OBJECT: Elevator **TIME LIMIT:** 10 minutes

CATHY BRETTELL: Breath sucks back into my throat—stomach ball jellies to my toes like an anchor hoisted over a ship—dull brass dragging thick fingers of midnight, current's chain unspools—like roller skates gliding freely—wind sassing back against stubborn waves, black fallen angels bow and thrash in the darkness—thunder twists between sweaty muscled clouds—silver daggers spear the sky horizon, lashing down at the warm sleeping distant halls—sandy upper lip catching foam of a root beer float—eyes widen—thirst deepens, a throat of parched earth guzzles a torpedo stream of charcoal water—stars mirror in the salty crystals—reeds bristle against oncoming Northern winds—smooth moonlit feathers hug against one bony leg for support—a white beam sweeps the coastal blanket—lighthouse calling a lone love—darkness capes around her tall slender body—urchins clinging, bottle bristles against her feet—sunrise begins to touch her—threads of melon flesh across cradled lids—shades of light lift the dreamy nightmare up—rolling it back into heaven's closet—soft crystal knob pulls shut … (time!)

SENSE-BOUND FREE ASSOCIATION

Think of object writing as sense-bound free association. As you can see from "Elevator," "Breath sucks back into my throat—stomach ball jellies to my toes like an anchor hoisted over ship" took Cathy from an elevator ride to an ocean storm, no permission asked.

There's no reason to stay loyal to the subject that sets you on your path. Your senses are driving the bus—you can go wherever they take you. The object you begin with might only be your starting point. Full right turns or leaps to other places are not only allowed but encouraged.

If you try to stay focused on the object you start with for the whole time, you may get bored with object writing after a few weeks. Let your hot morning shower with its rolling steam take you to thick clouds hanging overhead to the taste of rain to stomping through a puddle, splashing water up so it sprays like fireworks, to the boom in your chest and the smell of gunpowder and the taste of cotton candy.

Always stay with your senses, all seven of them. All within ten minutes. Don't worry about story lines or "how it really happened." No rhyme or rhythm. Not even full sentences. No one needs to understand where you are or how you got there. Save more focused writing for when you need to be focused.

Of course, instead of association, you certainly can stay within the framework of a story or event if you like, but let your senses drive the bus. As you remember the events, remember with your senses. How did the park smell? Were children giggling over by the duck pond? Italian sausages with steaming onions? Let us experience it too by engaging our senses: Stimulate us to see, smell, taste, hear, to really experience the story for ourselves.

Object writing is great fun. It prepares you for any creative writing you want to do: lyrics, poetry, short stories, novels. Great writing is full of sense-bound writing. There's a reason why the movie rarely seems as good as the book. The book created *your* movie, not someone else's.

GROUP WRITING

The fourteen-day challenges in this book work great in a group setting. You can expand your experience by asking friends to join you, either at your favorite coffee shop, someone's home, or even online. It's fascinating to hear other writers dive and roll off the same prompt. Get some people together, set a timer, and start with the object, person, time, or place—depending on the challenge of the day. When time is up, each person reads. Each of you will have something unique to offer. In a good group, the level of writing gets very high (or deep) very quickly.

(For additional reading on object writing, see chapter one of *Writing Better Lyrics*.)

Each day of the fourteen-day Object Writing challenge asks the reader to participate in three timed Object Writing exercises of five minutes, ten minutes and 90 seconds for fourteen days. To help inspire you, each day's object writing prompts will include two responses from other writers, including songwriters, poets, and prose writers. When you've finished, look at the example responses and dive in yourself, preferably in a special notebook or a separate file in your laptop.

Most of the responses in this first challenge are drawn from an object writing "contest" at objectwriting.com, a site built by Paul Penton in Melbourne, Australia. The contest ran for forty days, each day presenting a new prompt. We chose two, from the 20 to 40 responses we received each day, for inclusion here. This way, you'll have a group writing experience whether you form your own group or not.

But do form a group, or at least find a partner. It'll keep you on track.

The first five days are devoted to pure object writing. Let's call it "what" writing. Then three days each of "who," "when," and "where" writing. Have fun.

★ ★ ★ ★ ★

DAY #1

"WHAT" WRITING

Set a timer and respond to the following prompts for exactly the time allotted. Stop IMMEDIATELY when the timer goes off. Do not even finish the word you are on. Use only your seven senses. No judgments, comments, or quotes allowed. For the first few, feel free to read the samples before you begin. After a few days, read the samples after you've finished.

Use the list below as a place to let your eye wander when you're not sure where to go next.

Sight **Sound** **Taste** **Touch** **Smell** **Body** **Motion**

5 minutes: Sky

CATHY BRETTELL: Sapphires glisten underneath the glassine globe—marquise-shaped clouds floating, cross her eyes, back buried in the uncut summer grass—two yellow wings flash as she blinks, antennae curve and flutter like lashes upon her cheek. Roses billowing softly—pink lips pursing against cool violet petals—slender green stems bowing in her white hands like a hymnal, pages gilded—reflecting light like the crystal eyes of the lake—cattails sing, dragonflies passing between narrow rods of brown and white-fire—lazy slags of mud cup puddles of warm brine—salt drying white crusts at the slick edges—nighttime—worms guzzling their shade in the twiny albino roots—parasol dandelions ascend, scaling the blue heavens carrying child wishes …

PAT PATTISON: On my back, wind shadow in the grasses that bow in rhythm, tickling my face as I watch two redtails wheeling their figure 8's, riding, slicing the air—forewing feathers flattened against muscles and bone—peeling left toward a stand of sentinel pines brooding in shadow. Sun blanches my face, warm in speckles, rinsing clouds and lacing arrows of light against queen's lace and ragweed, ants scale weeds flattening in the wind …

Cathy takes you on quite a journey, moving beyond the girl, "back buried in the uncut summer grass, looking up at the sky," to the metaphor of the hymnal, which gives her something gilded to bring in the sun's shining on the lake, ending with "parasol dandelions … carrying child wishes." It's letting one thing roll into another, frequently leaving the original prompt fading somewhere in the dust.

Now, you try writing *Sky*.

10 minutes: Crash

SUSAN CATTANEO: Ear-splitting screech and then silence, the whine of steel against wood, the chrome fender like a blade against the rough neck of the old oak, the wound in the bark weeping sap and smelling of gasoline, a windshield reduced to glass pellets that crunch underfoot, a sneaker lies on its side near the licorice skid marks, its laces splayed like arms, the turn signal still blinking like beacon in the dark trees, the pines whisper carrying the faint smell of oil and gas and fear and perfume and beer, a sweaty hand fumbles for the doorknob, on hands and knees in the pine needles, the smell of overturned earth, neck muscles taunt and aching, he looks down at the red mark blossoming through his blue jeans and begins the feel the slow throb of pain, a heartbeat that pulses separate from his own heart, wiping the sweat from his upper lip, getting to his feet, the sky and stars and tree tops whirling in dizziness around him, he takes in great waves of air, trying to clear his head. he remembers the warm sticky counter at the bar, the smell of old peanuts and spilt beer, her voice like warm molasses, Jon Bon Jovi on the jukebox, and his wavy, ghostlike reflection in the mirror behind the cash register.

SCARLET KEYS: Pots slam on the floor again, they are her voice, doing the screaming that a nice southern woman can't do for herself. She smiles and pushes through that swinging wooden kitchen door every night as he mumbles like he's spitting out tobacco. She wipes her hands down the front of her flour-covered apron, slams the cupboards and seems to drop things pretty hard on that linoleum floor. She looks out the window, drinking iced sun tea, resting her arm on the faucet as she listens to it drip, shaken from her daydream like a lazy kid on Sunday morning clinging to the mattress as she hears him holler from the living room. His tone is so sharp it grabs her when he yells, as words fall hard on her heart like the pots on the floor. She strains to remember how he was when she first married him. He'd rush in the door and scoop her up like a handful of flowers and look at her. He'd breathe her in like he was going to drink …

How many senses has Susan made you use? Remember, the more senses you involve, the more real your reader's experience becomes. Both Susan and Scarlet use interesting simile and metaphor. (Much more on that as we move through these challenges.)

Object writing is pretty flexible. Susan stayed at an actual car crash. Scarlet crashes pots on the linoleum floor. Both stay focused on one scene, as I did in "Sky," while Cathy takes you floating away on a carpet of free association. The only rule: Stay attached to your senses.

Your turn. Give *Crash* a try.

90 seconds: Lily Pad

CATHY BRETTELL: Backs of hands grown over with emerald moss—rocking chair webbed with rickety spider legs—ponytail—wire gray hair like a witch's broom—Cutlery limps across her throat—bones like bridges suspending wrinkled skin—red pools under the Wood-Spoke Linoleum …

PAT PATTISON: Glittering in sunlight, swamp grass and green algae dance. A V-ing above the largemouth's wake, widening to the shore, a mouth gulping stars, galaxies seen in the eyes of a child.

Pretty intense, these ninety-second dashes. They'll really build your speed and get you deep into your senses quickly. And, they're fun. Your turn.

DAY #2
"WHAT" WRITING

Okay, one day down. You've had the experience of timed, sense-bound writing. The more you do it, and the more consistently you do it, the better you'll get. It just takes practice, like anything else. As you're writing, keep asking, "What's that like?" "Can I get more specific?" "Is there another sense I could be using?"

Once again, set a timer and respond to the prompts for exactly the time allotted. Stop IMMEDIATELY when the timer goes off.

Use the list below as a place to let your eye wander when you're not sure where to go next.

Sight **Sound** **Taste** **Touch** **Smell** **Body** **Motion**

5 minutes: Bathroom Mirror

ADAM FARR: Like a silver fridge door, seen through stray wafts of shower steam. I am a huddling shadow, arms franticly trying to de-damp a ghostlike body emerging from a rain forest into an igloo. I am tense like a frosty washing line waiting for the expanding sun to bring relaxation. A rounded fruit shampoo smell is the only colour in the dark morning. Tentative toe tips approach the sink across the bed of icy tile nails. My jaw is stone.

Small tears show that the mirror is not dead. I watch their jerky progress. Stop—silence—drop. My features start to become visible. Relieved, the world and I re-enter each other's existence.

SAM ALESSI: The shower steam rolls in swirls against the bathroom mirror as I step out of the shower. The floor feels cold to my warm toes. I see beads of water forming and jumping their ways down the mirror like the cylinders in my car trying to get up to speed to meet the day. I feel rushed inside, ahead of my body that is only shown in patches in the mirror, link to some cyborg refugee planted here in this lost place. The smell of peppermint hangs in the air, swirling with the cloud of shower steam. I flip on the fan to clear the fog, the rattle is disturbing but fits my inner rush much better than the calm of my morning heat bath. I stop for a moment, turn off the fan, and feel the room around me, cool breezes move over my skin, the mirror has cleared enough to see the dripping hair, the whiskers trying to grow, the body that well ... I got to pee then run ...

Both Sam and Adam engage multiple senses besides sight: touch, body, sound, smell, and even motion in Sam's "I stop for a moment, turn off the fan, and feel the room around me, cool breezes move over my skin." Nice of them to invite readers into their morning bathrooms.

Now, you try.

10 minutes: Dentist

SUSAN CATTANEO: clenching and unclenching my hands, nails making half-moon shapes in my palms, a dizzy heat in my face and my heart galloping in my chest, she pulls back my lips—they stretch like old rubber bands that might snap, Olivia Newton John's greatest hits on the tinny speaker in the ceiling, rubber gloves smelling like beach balls and the blood slowly rising to my head as the chair is dipped backwards, the sound of the drill running around in my head like a rabid hamster on an exercise wheel, willing the cemented muscles in my neck to relax, thoughts careening away from the idyllic white beach in my "relaxing space" and making a head-on collision with images of long metal hooks scraping down to nerves as pale and delicate as baby's hair, taste of pennies in my mouth, the cotton roll is a gag, my tongue like a forlorn lover longs to caress the tooth but is held back by the tube sucking on my saliva, the machine gurgles like a patient on life-support ...

SHANE ADAMS: He's scraping my teeth ... a coat hanger dragging its fingernail on the forehead of my molar. Tooth decay hides in the moist nooks of my dental canyon, like dark green echoes of plaque and popcorn shells. The dentist is lower, close to my face, his own mouth hidden behind the clipper ship sail of a breathing mask. I'd like to lean up and bite his nose. Shoot upwards like a corpse on springs, but the suction tube holds me back, drinking my spittle and drying my mouth like a terry cloth question mark. The drill bit burns my teeth. I can smell it. Burning pine cones that blossom and spill their pine nuts like a bag of sesame seeds. Is that smoke coming from my mouth? Or dust? The light hovering over me like an upside down toilet is blinding me. Even when I close my eyes I can see its fluorescent donut hovering on the black membrane of my closed eyelid. I turn to spit. My tongue tastes like a garden slug. The white foam of my spit laps over my bottom lip and hangs like a clock's pendulum or a glistening teardrop-shaped spider swaying under a garden trellis.

A lot of this book is about using metaphor and simile effectively. You can see why from Susan and Shane here. Both take you into the dentist's chair and hold you there for the duration. You see, hear, taste, smell, feel tension, feel confined, not only because of they're so locked into sense-bound language, but because of their use of metaphor. Patience.

Your turn.

90 seconds: Screwdriver

PAUL PENTON: Yellow handle with black strokes, silver-pointed jabbing tool, chrome shaft, my face reflected in the steel, fitting into the slot, the groove, pressure on my palm pushing through like deliverance, twisting upper arm muscles straining to go that one last turn. The freshly cut pine smelling sweet and new like being in nature, axes wielded, chainsaws buzzing on the breeze ...

JOY GORA: A pile of rocky cubes climb into the bottom of my glass. They sharply crack as a smooth splash of vodka plunges to the bottom. Sweetly soothed by the cascading orange juice, the ice swims freely. The chilled metal tumbler caps the rim and with one deliberate shake my weekend begins. I spin and swirl the cherry red swizzle stick and draw ...

I like Paul's use of the organic (body) sense, and Joy's interesting angle, inviting readers for a dip in her glass.

Your turn.

DAY #3

"WHAT" WRITING

By now you should be more aware of the power of multiple senses to make an experience more real and engaging. Polling your various senses as you write is a pretty effective way to keep an idea rolling. And remember, writing from your senses not only invites your readers into their own sense world (making *your* writing about *them*), but more important, it makes the act of writing more stimulating and real to you. And the more senses you use, the more dizzying your carousel ride becomes.

Set a timer and respond to the following prompts for exactly the time allotted. Stop IMMEDIATELY when the timer goes off.

Sight   Sound   Taste   Touch   Smell   Body   Motion

5 minutes: Umbrella

KAZ MITCHELL: Fumbling with the release catch, in a hurry to get under the wide rim of the umbrella as quickly as possible. Hail hammering against the pavements, icy pellets stinging my face. Whoosh, and suddenly the webbed beast sprung from his cocoon and caught me by surprise. I jump and exclaim a loud swear word as the wind …

MO MCMORROW: With a whoosh and a snap and a rush of cold rain the umbrella's skirt is blown up and I'm pulled rudely along the sidewalk grasping onto the thin metal leg as if holding the foot of someone being swept away in a storm. Water lashes my face and runs down under my nose into my mouth. Salt. My legs run to catch up with the rest of me like a comedian and I sneak a glance around to see if there's a laughing audience. Suddenly the umbrella closes shut in the reversing wind and my legs pedal backward to catch up the other way. My stomach lurches and I feel a tingling in my head like my skin is preparing for a sudden impact.

I like Kaz's "icy pellets stinging my face" and her umbrella as a "webbed beast." And Mo's "umbrella's skirt is blown up" is a treat. Note their use of multiple senses.

Now, you give it a try.

10 minutes: Hair

GILLIAN WELCH: Silky strands in clumps and clips in bolts and plaits in pigtails and ponytails tied up in bright elastic rubber bands like bunches of parsley, sprouting out of her head like Athena, like antennae, like antlers for the female of the species. Really dirty hair smells like gear oil, like the darkened sweat bands of old hats, shady and musky oily dusky leather and sweat smell and with straw hats mildewed hay, like a denim jacket after being in the park all day. Clean hair is soapy silky, too soft too stay in place it slips and slides away a sly smiling child, taunting teasing testing. Shining like taffeta in those colors that have no name. A hundred shades of platinum is my true lover's hair. A hundred shades of silver and gold are hidden there. But you would call it brown.

SUSAN CATTANEO: Delicate strands plastered to skin, golden tentacles wrapping like snakes around sweaty shoulders, bodies pulsing to the incessant beat of the music, hands raised up as if in prayer to the revolving disco ball, smell of Marlboro cigarettes, taffy-colored pink nails drum on the bar counter, spandex and eye shadow the color of antifreeze, slathering Bonne Bell lip gloss on each lip, smelling of strawberries and red licorice, the hair teased and coaxed by the spitting hairspray, a comb shucking the strands of hair the way you shuck corn, the hairspray smells sweet and toxic, the tattoo of my aunt's pink coral lipstick on the end of a slim Parliament cigarette, long black gloves stuffed into a genuine alligator purse, I hide amongst the fur coats in the coat closet, the smell of camphor laced with perfume, hearing my brother breathing fast as he tiptoes past the closed door, hunting me down, suppressing a giggle as the fur tickles my nose, a sneeze creeps its way up my throat, I try and swallow, today's tuna fish sandwich lingers …

After you've finished yours, go back to these and pick out the phrases you like best. Try answering the question, "Why do you like those best?" It will help you discover tools for your own writing.

90 seconds: Feather

KAZ MITCHELL: Seagull feather blowing through the breeze brushes against my skin. Breathing in the salty sea breeze. The greasy smell of fish and chips. Smudges on my fingers from the newspaper wrappings.

DEBORAH QUILTER: Tickled under the chin by a matted pearl and slate feather from a farmyard duck.

Bumbling over a pail of eggs by the henhouse and sliding into a trickle of yolks …

I like that both Kaz and Deborah move freely from *feather* into fish and chips, and broken eggs, respectively. The only rule here is to stay sense-bound, so keeping to a single focus isn't necessary. Practicing this kind of sensual free-association will help you brainstorm more effectively.

Your turn.

DAY #4
"WHAT" WRITING

Three days down. You're almost becoming a veteran. As you're discovering, there are no rules here. You can stay focused on an event or experience, or you can float from place to place, rolling off one idea onto the next. Just stay with your senses.

Set your timer and respond to the following prompts for exactly the time allotted. Stop IMMEDIATELY when the timer goes off.

Sight Sound Taste Touch Smell Body Motion

5 minutes: Curb

NICK MILLER: Foot sliding off the side of the curb, scraping fine cement dust. Wind from cars rocks me, car horns drone by as sunlight blazes off too-hot-to-the-touch metal. Too hot like the sand down at the beach, you run and try to let your feet touch down for just a second. Skin sun drenched, like you're marinated in sun wine. Another summer passing like a long wave which takes forever to break, collecting more memories … you start dreaming

LINDA M: Flaking cracked yellow paint clings to the curb like a skin disease. Diesel drops drizzle like rain, a cold concrete slap on the face. Red balloons trigger panic and obstruction, tripping hard, toe-stubbing confusion and puddle jumping, zigzag. White powder tickles my nose as I fall face first into screaming traffic and twisted panic bites hard, ripping soft skin wide open.

Check out Nick and Linda's verbs. Go ahead, underline them. I'll wait.

Strong verbs are the key to strong writing. Audition your verbs. Let them prance and somersault for you. Verbs based in metaphor or steeped in the senses usually get the gig.

Now write about your own curb.

10 minutes: Bouquet

GILLIAN WELCH: The stems are molding in the dark of the vase, rotten, down out of sight filling the house with musty funk. The petals are on the table, an I Ching telling me of the haste of my departure. The litter box is full of cat shit and the ammonia of the cat urine hits my nose in an acid wave when I round the corner into the kitchen. Cat puke on the carpet upstairs like a dead little rodent lying under the window. Closed up house smells of hot attic. Somehow the colors all shift when you go away and come back. Dishes in the sink look like archeological dig crusted and smeared in ancient browns. What can we learn from these people? They lived with animals. Burnt out lightbulbs and softened oranges greet me and tell me I have work to do just to keep my head above water cause there is a slow leak in this lifeboat and a week away means some emergency bailing. I am bailing. I am taking out the ripe and evolving garbage under the sink.

SHANE ADAMS: The preschool kids are a bouquet of flowers playing tag on a baseball field. Their water balloons are rubbery comets bursting like wet tattoos on their delightfully screaming backsides. Diamond patterns of freshly mowed grass shine like a chessboard in the summer afternoon while parents laugh from the sidelines like balloon-filling and knee-bandaging coaches. One of the children, a girl with a kickball-red bathing suit, stops to pick a dandelion. Its white Afro is a sunburst of seeds that she blows towards the sun … but the seeds return like cotton boomerangs and alight in her hair and tickle the ridge of her nose like dainty paratroopers. She tosses the used stem over her tan shoulder like a botanical grenade pin and runs to her mom who brushes her hair back with the swipe of a left hand and a pat to her bottom. From nowhere, sprinklers pop to the surface and strafe the giggling crowd. A hundred hands instantaneously are held out like impotent shields to block the clicking spray as fathers scramble with the folding picnic tables whose Jell-O salads duck and bounce like mandarin orange patients on wooden stretchers. Every child's legs ...

Now, it's your turn.

90 seconds: Rain Cloud

KAZ MITCHELL: Out on the moors, thick with bristling heather. Wind hurtles down from the mountains freezing the tip of my nose, carrying with it the damp odour of a storm brewing. Fat rain clouds spreading across the sky blotting out all chance of a ...

ADAM FARR: I feel the sharp cold of the thin air peeling at my face. The moisture clings like to a shared towel that never quite shakes off the damp. My breath is fresh and alive in comparison, pausing to consider the rocky terrain and then swallowed by the exploded ocean.

Try it yourself. I hope that paying attention to your verbs helped your writing today. It's a surefire way to take your writing to another level instantly.

DAY #5

"WHAT" WRITING

Congratulations for staying on board so far. This is the last day of "what" writing, writing from objects or things, which has been the staple diet of object writers for years and has spawned some pretty remarkable writing. It gives you a place to start and a specific focus for your journey through or from an object.

Set a timer and respond to the following prompts for exactly the time allotted. Stop IMMEDIATELY when the timer goes off

Sight Sound Taste Touch Smell Body Motion

5 minutes: Movie Theater

KAZ MITCHELL: The rustling of greasy fingers amongst salty popcorn, the sweet smell opening up my memory box to reveal a snaking queue on a balmy summer's evening. A threadbare carpet greets us as we scamper indoors, the thrill of the movies catching our breath. A constellation of glittering movie stars across the screen …

SHIRLEY TO: Carefully walking up the stairs, listening to the sticky squeaky sound the bottom of my shoes make with each step, glazed slightly with spilled soda and artificial sweetener, I find my seat and squeeze past the couple who look like they have been stationed in the theater for a long time. I reach for the cloth-covered seat and push it down and slowly slide onto it, it makes a sound like the screws and hinges are complaining of waking them from their sweet dreams. The advertisements are showing, flashing red and green and white light, trying to wake up the stale air in this big room. The air is choked with the smell of popcorn, the fake butter syrup thing that has been lavishly poured onto the little celebration of fireworks of corn. The smell makes me want to vomit. Popcorn, it's soggy and doesn't taste like corn. But kettle corn—the crunchy sweetness that explodes in my mouth, waking up my taste buds, my mouth watery. Trailer, deep voice is …

Hot spots: "A constellation of glittering movie stars." "The air is choked with the smell of popcorn."

See what you come up with.

10 minutes: Cigar

SUSAN CATTANEO: As the flames lick their wrinkled feet, smoke like fog rises up and swirls in the air overhead, glasses of cut crystal gleam from the bar, the smell of oiled leather, smoke, and cologne. He leans back against the mud-red leather seat, bow tie tucked like a napkin under his chin. His breath is laced with bourbon and tobacco, the conversation drifts like a raft in the sea of smoke, stock tips slither from his overwet lips as his brain scrambles and stumbles to remember which story he told the wife tonight. Working late or dinner with the client? Confidence pools in his chest like an oil slick. He knows both women wait for him, patient as sheep, longing for the crunch of his tires on gravel in the driveway and the burnt musky smell of cigar on his lips. The wife drowns in neglect, ears impaled with diamonds but her heart is empty and echoing. The girlfriend lies in her spacious bleach white minimalist apartment. A tsunami of boredom washes over her that only his platinum Amex card can staunch.

ANTHONY CESERI: Watching the end turn bright red as his chest lifts upwards from his deep breath. Then smoke billows out of his mouth, as he removes the cigar and floods the space in front of him. Smoke pouring out past his lips as if a dam burst. The smell clouds the room. You can smell the bitter brown cigar stank in the air. I can almost taste the wet paper on my tongue as I breathe in the cigar-laden air.

When the quieter moments align with another one of his puffs, you can hear the crackling of the brown paper as it's burned up with another one of his big inhales. The tip gets red again, and then leaves its ashy remains behind. The smoke stings my eyes. They feel as if the insides of my eyelids are dry, and made of sandpaper. Then they start to water.

I imagine what the cigar feels like in his fingers. Warm, and rough to the touch. Leaving a noticeable smell on his hands that won't come off before multiple showers. But of course he'll have had more cigars by then anyway … keeping the cycle alive.

Now I watch him take his last puff and smash his stub down into the glass ashtray. Hearing the ashes shift around against the glass as he crushes them down. The butt stands upright, with smoke pouring upward as he walks away.

Look at Susan's "conversation drifts like a raft in the sea of smoke, stock tips slither from his overwet lips" and Anthony's "Smoke pouring out past his lips as if a dam burst." Both writers appeal to multiple senses and soak you in the smoky room.

Now, you try.

90 seconds: Arrow

NELSON BOGART: Poison-tipped rail of death, smells like the fire it was forged in, flying swiftly into the dark, at the silhouette sitting by the smoking fire, unaware of anything except the snap of a branch and the sound of the bowstring twa …

LINDA M: Cupid clips a wing, thrusts a limping arrow through a grain of sand. Saltwater taffy laughed down my throat and tickled my tummy lining, a frantic fish flopping, a worm winding through my metallic veins …

Nelson focuses on a moment and takes you right there with a mix of sight, smell, and sound. Linda bounds away from the arrow into her tummy and organic sense. Either works. Both stimulate your senses productively.

Your turn.

DAY #6
"WHO" WRITING

It's fair to say that object writing, as you've experienced it in this book so far, is "what" writing. Like "elevator," *things* are your starting point, your diving board. There are other possibilities, too, especially *who, when,* and *where.* The fourteen-day challenge asks you to explore all four as the days roll on. Now, rather than working with objects, you'll try "who" writing —looking at, or through, the eyes of specific characters.

"Who" writing is great for character development. In every song, you have to answer the questions: Who is talking? Who is she talking to? Sometimes the character is pretty much you, talking either to the audience or to a particular person. Sometimes it's not. Either way, keep the character in focus. Practice creating characters with specific attitudes.

Use other perspectives. Your object writing can be from the perspective of an airline flight attendant, hurrying to serve drinks on a short flight. Or a volunteer at an animal rescue shelter. A car thief, as in Sting's "Stolen Car" or his "Tomorrow We'll See," from the perspective of a male prostitute.

People watching is full of interesting possibilities. Ask yourself questions: "Does she play golf? When did she learn?" "What was his favorite game when he was little?" Of course, you'll be drawing on your own experiences as you answer your questions. And always stay close to your senses. Specifics. Sense images.

I also recommend this kind of storytelling when hanging out with other writers. You might even make a special trip to the mall or the airport to exercise your powers of observation. (I call it the "airport game.") As somebody passes you, ask your friend a question:

"Who did he take to his junior prom?" "Does she get along with her younger sister?" Take turns asking questions.

You'll be doing "who" writing for the next three days. Have fun.

Set a timer and respond to the following prompts for exactly the time allotted. Stop IMMEDIATELY when the timer goes off.

Sight Sound Taste Touch Smell Body Motion

5 minutes: Sailor

KAZ MITCHELL: At sea, the wind flapping his clothes against his skin, making him feel alive. Breathing in the salty air like it was his lifeline, the antidote to city smog and the hustle of corporate life. Tasting this freedom with relish, as if it were a banquet for kings, a smile spreads across his stubble-ridden face as wide as the Arc de Triomphe. The sails stretch out towards the heavens, rattling against the mast and sounding as grand as a Beethoven concerto.

TANJA WARD: The mermaid tattoo spread over his whole back. The mermaid seemed to be smiling, although with age. Her tail, abnormally long, blue faded to light gray on her tail. The full lips once perfectly fire red faded to burnt orange. As he lay on the table the mermaid seemed almost asleep and I could smell the ocean drifting around his body. His skin, raped by too many sunburns to count.

I got to know both of these sailors: the executive out on the bay and the aging sea-worn sailor, body fading like the mermaid's. By noting something specific, their character evolves quickly. Have you read Malcolm Gladwell's *Blink*?

Write about your own sailor.

10 minutes: Waitress Clearing a Table

DEBORAH QUILTER: A wobbly fan circles above servings of unfinished breakfast. Rosanna spritzes the vinyl ketchup-and-mayonnaise-checkered table cover. The floor is sticky with syrupy sludge from the iced drink machine that twirls a cocktail of passion and punch. Rosanna piles up the plates; sodden crusts of cornbread, maple and egg yolk, lights a cigarette and lets her lipstick and soft bite hold it in place. She wraps a clean cotton apron around her waist in a bow, stretching pink latex gloves over her smooth hands and filling the sink with soaking suds. She pins a rose under her hairclip and rustles a straggly bunch of curls into a knot, turns the knob of the radio to a flush of flamenco and starts to slowly move her hips as she scrapes and scrubs. The morning fog is clearing out of the bay, the sun fumbling through. She pours a strong coffee, inhaling the fumes ...

JOHN O'SHAUGHNESSY: Wobble wobble, cups and plates, spoons and coffee dancing to the orchestrated sliding of swollen feet under blue-veined pylons swirling through the tobacco haze and idle chatter, bending to the slurping, dripping, mouth-dabbing hoi polloi littering the footpath between the drab facade of the bank and the retro-wear clothes shop, haunting the sticky, cracked pavement. She slips the greasy coin into the wishing-well apron pocket and moves seamlessly to the next table, eyes reflecting nothing of self-betrayal or the shallow conversation and miserly intentions of the patrons.

I love Rosanna: "She pins a rose under her hairclip and rustles a straggly bunch of curls into a knot, turns the knob of the radio to a flush of flamenco and starts to slowly move her hips as she scrapes and scrubs." And John's "She slips the greasy coin into the wishing-well apron pocket." Both Deborah and John let the reader observe their waitresses—they *show* them in action. In getting to know them from the outside, it becomes possible to write from inside, too, *through* their eyes. You should take a shot at it.

90 seconds: Priest

PAUL PENTON: White collar, leaning over, praying. Swishing around a container of incense. On the pulpit, thundering voice of god, hands and fists smashing the air, congregation in compartmentalized rows like a housing estate, the words of god flying out of his mouth like arrows. Never married, never known the pleasure of oneness except with god. Alone.

JOY GORA: Wisdom lines framing blue eyes and pearly wavy hair tossed to the side. A soft black robe scented with incense as a bell chimes high. A dry, thin wafer turns to pasty mush to be washed down with tart red wine sipped from an old ornate cup. Air thick with devotion ...

Hot spots: "A dry, thin wafer turns to pasty mush to be washed down with tart red wine ..." "Congregation in compartmentalized rows like a housing estate."

Now, your turn.

DAY #7

"WHO" WRITING

I hope your first day of "who" writing opened some new possibilities, maybe motivating you to do some extra writing on your own. Here we go again.

Set a timer and respond to the following characters for exactly the time allotted. Stop IMMEDIATELY when the timer goes off.

Sight Sound Taste Touch Smell Body Motion

5 minutes: Balloon Man

SCOTT WILKINSON: In the park, the sun warms my back like I'm bathing in a delicate dripping, soothing coat of warm fudge. The peculiar combination smell of cotton candy, caramel popcorn and mechanic's lubricating oil lacing the air. One child laughing on the tiny race-car ride. The teenagers curdling screams on the monster drop. The balloon man standing in full array of colors. A kindly smile, and helium tanks straddle his makeshift shop. Blue, red, yellow, purple and green float above his head. The children flock and request their color. The smiles, the thrill of a balloon tied to their wrist floating above their head, sugar candy dribbling down the side of their mouth and the air filled with a symphony of laughter and sweet sugary smell, spell pure joy.

MO MCMORROW: Practicing for hours in the old living room back on Park St. I stretch the balloon lip over the orange plastic pump and make like I was inflating a tire. The balloon stretches and lengthens in seconds and with a flupping sound I pull the balloon off and struggle to tie a knot breathing shallow. Sometimes I tighten it with my teeth and get the sharp rubber taste on my tongue. Twist the balloon, studying the book the whole time and counting the twists, I hold my breath and squint my eyes because of all the others that have exploded in my face. They're slippery and powdery and threaten to snap but I keep thinking of the guy at the fair that is always stuffing money in his pockets and the smell of popcorn and gunpowder ...

Try writing about your own balloon man.

10 minutes: Homeless Child

CATRINA SEIFFERT: A weary face peers from the weathered car window. Old tears have worn track marks down her dusty cheeks. She stares blankly at the drizzle ignoring the sunny voices of the morning radio and heaves her sweatered chest in a heavy sigh. Her stomach gurgles without her usual crunchy bowl of cornflakes and she squints while imagining a plate of honeyed toast piled high to the car roof.

The five-year-old thuds back into the vinyl seat. Her left hand twirls her dirty blond curls around her finger and then into her strawberry lips. A miniature river of saliva runs down her chin as she smells the fries from the corner drive-in. The rain plays a soundtrack of fairy drums on the car roof. A drowned sparrow shakes its sodden wings ...

MO MCMORROW: Dirty bare feet, skinny little legs bruised but wiry strong, a soiled dress, once pink with darker flowers of some color, arms thin and reaching out, an expression that kicks me right in the gut. Her dark eyes are sad; I slip money from my pocket and hold it flapping in the air. She leaps for it like a monkey and scurries away behind the fence. I hear scuffling sounds and whispers between the pilings of the fence. I peek around at a little huddled mass of tiny limbs and three sets of black eyes looking up at me like abandoned kittens in a box. The scent of fermenting garbage knocks me back a pace. A sharp taste rises in my throat and I swallow hard then open my mouth to breathe. I stoop down and they back away like one creature.

Wonderful portraits from both Catrina and Mo. Catrina's third-person point of view allows a look into the child's mind "imagining a plate of honeyed toast piled high to the car roof." Mo's first-person narrative provides interactions with the three children. Nice verbs in both pieces. Now, your turn.

90 seconds: Trucker

LEORA NOSKO: Bare hands, stale beer breath, furrowed brow and sweat-stained foam hat. His body sunk deep into the torn vinyl seat, strong arm wrestler grip on the long stick shift. Motor vibrations pass rapidly through his thick form and around the humming cabin.

CATRINA SEIFFERT: He heaves his heavy body out of the driver's seat swishing the sticky flies off his dusty face. His faded blue singlet soaked up the sweat in patches under his pungent armpits.

Both truckers are sweaty. Great details abound in Leora's piece, especially the motor vibrations. I like the faded blue singlet. He's fading, too.

The details you use say something about the character you're describing. Remember Tanja's mermaid tattoo? Try it out.

DAY #8

"WHO" WRITING

This is your last day of "who" writing. Dig in.

Set a timer and respond to the following characters for exactly the time allotted. Stop IMMEDIATELY when the timer goes off.

Sight Sound Taste Touch Smell Body Motion

5 minutes: Cyclist

MANUEL STÜBINGER: Airstream hoists the whole body, as if I take off, take wing. I whoosh over paving and tar, wreaths singing. Palms burn from tight grasp on the rubber handle. Pressure of the saddle, fire in the thighs, breathlessness in the chest. Tilting into the curve. Fragrant spring flies around me, smell the river-bed, green and fresh …

TASLEEM RAJWANI: Thin spinning wheels. Spokes and speed and tires treading against the wet pavement. Rain slaps against the biker's knees as he races home in only a T-shirt and a pair of spandex shorts. Sweat and raindrops mix together to form a freshness that cools and tingles his legs and elbows. Hairs sticking up, but clothes sticking close to his skin. A dark blue helmet protects his head from dampness and drizzle that drips off of branches and awnings and umbrellas of people who don't look up to see who they are hitting while they pass. There is a black umbrella, tattered and broken lying in the middle of the sidewalk. Its folds look like a sleeping bat, blind to all those passing by. Pitter-patter of feet and sloshing of black dress shoes in the puddles in front of the business district. High rises appear to touch the clouds …

Manuel writes from inside the biker, Tasleem from outside. As an experiment, try reversing them: Read Manuel's in third person ("as *he* takes off …") and read Tasleem's in first person ("Rain slaps against *my* knees as *I* race …"). Is there a difference in tone and immediacy?

Now try reading both in second person, using *you* instead of *I* or *he*.

> Airstream hoists the whole body, as if you take off, take wing. You whoosh over paving and tar, wreaths singing.

Note that, in second person, commands are possible, so you could eliminate the subject from the second sentence:

> Airstream hoists the whole body, as if you take off, take wing. Whoosh over paving and tar, wreaths singing.

Pretty cool. Now, your turn.

10 minutes: Ballerina

CHANELLE DAVIS: I can hear my breath, quick, shallow, electric current in my blood, heart beating almost through my skin. A soft constant drone of conversation behind the heavy royal-red curtains. Clapping, loud like storm rain, makes my feet move, soft silk shoes gliding along the smooth black stage floor. Spotlights beam from over my head and shine down, reflecting off my satin dress. Up on my toes, curling them and stretching long arms, tipping over left then right, arching my back, feeling skin move over my ribs, rippling, inhaling deep. Spinning to the orchestra, violins soar and I fall to my knees, head down, cheek pressed to the cold floor and wait, still. The lights dim, I close my eyes. Can taste my lip gloss, strawberry. He comes to my side, the smell of cologne in the air as he grabs my hand and pulls me to his chest, smooth and tanned arms, drums start pulsing …

SUSAN ANDERS: Sweat, kneading the knobs formed on her toes, calluses, leather skin on feet hammered by point shoes. The silky satin of the scuffed shoes, then the rough turtle skin of her feet. she squeezes her feet back into the shoes, they smell of dirt and sweat, laces them up. Stands and begins her routine, the clomp as her feet fall with each leap, the crrrrrr as her clothes sweep with her, her panting, a hundred muscles crying out with each controlled bend and sweep of her leg, then arm, then leg again. She watches each move in the mirror, sees the little tremors of exhausted muscles that she must control, her mouth firm, no, betrays pain, relax it, another turn, she watches her right hand and adjusts her index finger by the tiniest of curls. Onward, she tastes metal and realizes that she's bitten her tongue while concentrating, blood. She smiles just slightly. She watches herself again, sees a hunched up crone galomping around a room full of mirrors and wood floors and walls, then sees a lioness slowly approaching the kill, then sees shoots from a dandelion wafting …

Try the point-of-view experiment again here. Do Chanelle's from both third and second person; do Susan's from first and second person. Again, be alert in second person for commands and questions.

90 seconds: Puppy

PAUL PENTON: Big eyes looking up like glass marbles. Tail wagging back and forth in a seesaw. Running in jumbled heap, legs uncoordinated. A fawn blob of fur and fluff, eager, happy. Warm puppy breath with lizard tongue that licks my face, high-pitched yaps and barks of excitement. Paws scrabbling across shiny tiles in bathroom tissue commercials—cute!

HOLLY BRETTELL: On the car ride home the puppy is whining, pawing and fogging up the window with his breath. Your heart is pounding with excitement seeing your little one padding down the unfamiliar hallway, trying to find a place to mark his territory. You rush him outside not thinking of the potty-training process. New toys cover the floor. After a long hard day as he drifts off, his breathing getting slower, you don't care about the mess around the corner, this moment is too precious—his first nap in his new home.

Both Paul and Chanelle use multiple senses. Nice puppies. Try it yourself.

That's it, eight days down, six to go. You've looked at objects ("what") and characters ("who"), and have seen how they can interact with each other. Objects reveal character; character assembles objects. It's a wonderful, fluid dance. All it takes is practice.

DAY #9

"WHEN" WRITING

Welcome to "when" writing. It will give you practice locating your characters and the objects around them at various times.

"When" can be seasonal—"across the morning sky, all the birds are leaving." It can be a time of day—"midnight at the oasis," or even special occasion: "Chestnuts roasting on an open fire." Play around with it.

Setting a time of day or year adds a new dimension to your writing. There's a vast difference between the following three versions:

> I looked at her, she looked back at me …
>
> A sunny morning, I looked at her, she looked back at me …
>
> A cold winter, I looked at her, she looked back at me ..,
>
> Our skin wrinkled with age, I looked at her, she looked back at me …

There's lots of stimulation available in "when," as you'll see. Watch the ideas tumble out.

Set a timer and respond to the following prompts for exactly the time allotted. Stop IMMEDIATELY when the timer goes off.

Sight Sound Taste Touch Smell Body Motion

5 minutes: Summer Rainstorm

LINDA M: Clapping clouds lick warm wind and drizzle dewy rain on the tart green grass below. Wet dirt cushions my feet, daisy sprays tickle my ankle like a bracelet of watery charms. Sun soaks through the drops, an aqua-coloured rainbow bends across the hopeful horizon like childhood prayers and plastic rosaries …

DEBORAH QUILTER: Billowing steam rose from the asphalt as the warm rain tapped down on the melted black surface. Veins of lightning splintered across the skyline and a city of umbrellas popped open. Dirty dark clouds clustered overhead threatening to bucket down in pellets. Sticky skin plunged into goose bumps and slippery feet skittles. Traffic slowed to a spluttering slosh, windscreen wipers batted the rain away and beaming car lights flashed along afternoons' dirty streets. The pavements filled with pot-holed puddles …

The prompt specifies summer, but Deborah takes the writing even further into "when" with "beaming car lights flashed along afternoons' dirty streets."

Check out both Linda and Deborah's verbs. Yum.

One other thing: Note that Deborah's description is in past tense, removing the reader a bit from the scene. (It happened, after all, in the past.) Look what happens in present tense:

> Billowing steam rises from the asphalt as the warm rain taps down on the melted black surface. Veins of lightning splinter across the skyline and a city of umbrellas pops open. Dirty dark clouds cluster overhead threatening to bucket down in pellets. Sticky skin plunges into goose bumps and slippery feet skittles. Traffic slows to a spluttering slosh, windscreen wipers bat the rain away and beaming car lights flash along afternoons' dirty streets. The pavements fill with pot-holed puddles …

Pretty big difference. Present tense is more immediate than past tense or future tense—not that everything you write needs to be immediate. Just remember that tense is a tool—a choice you make. Don't let the fact that it happened in the past make you write it in past tense. Don't let "how it really happened" drive the bus. You're the writer.

And it's your turn.

10 minutes: Graduation

CHANELLE DAVIS: Parading down the main street of town, spilling onto the road, hundreds of graduates in black flowing gowns and hats with tassles swinging, blue and white collars, descending on the theatre. Sun heating up, burning through our gowns, sweat on my face, big smiles and laughter, whooping and shouting, skipping, I feel my high heels on the footpath, clicking, a street full of friends, flicking through the programme looking for my name, hearing it called and walking up on stage, carefully, follow the white line on the floor, around the towering bouquets of white and blue flowers, shake hands firmly with the man and pose for a photograph, routine clapping, hands sore and red. Listening to speakers and Maori blessings, calls, some students dressed in Korowai, native bird feathered cloaks handed down …

DEBORAH QUILTER: Felt tasseled caps and camera clicks of smiles. Soft clapping hands and back-patting laudatory gestures. Doves of freedom flying toward the open door that swings beside a cliff. Holding grip of rolling scrolls tied in satin ribbons. Handshake gowns, handed down, fresh and pressed as new. Bumbled words spill out amongst champagnes gulping clatter. Pleased as punch, parents toast to the marvel of their making. Muted nights of muddled minds that cram before the morning. Blurred new days that fade away into late-night library ramblings. Friendships made and promises accidentally broken. Textbook trash heaps, lonesome walk back home. On solid the ravens flock …

Both Chanelle and Deborah remain in the present, making the experience more immediate. As an experiment, translate both into past tense. Note that both use a lot of the *ing* form of the verb, which is tense-neutral. Look:

> Parading down the main street of town, spilling onto the road, hundreds of graduates in black flowing gowns and hats with tassels swinging, blue and white collars, descending on the theater …

So far, there's no tense established. It could be:

> Parading down the main street of town, spilling onto the road, hundreds of graduates in black flowing gowns and hats with tassles swinging, blue and white collars, descending on the theater, the graduating class looked fabulous …

It also could be:

> Parading down the mainstreet of town, spilling onto the road, hundreds of graduates in black flowing gowns and hats with tassles swinging, blue and white collars, descending on the theater, the graduating class will look fabulous.

Chanelle doesn't put the reader clearly in present tense until line four, "I feel … ." Deborah's first commitment to present tense is also in her fourth line, "Bumbled words spill out … ." Tense-neutral verbs can be very useful. For more, see chapter nine in *Writing Better Lyrics*, "Stripping Your Repetition for Re-painting."

Your turn.

90 seconds: Wedding Rehearsal Dinner

KAZ MITCHELL: The champagne is crisp and full of bubble, just like the chatter around the table. There is much joyous banter and rubbing of shoulders as the guests warm to each other, over hot slices of roasted chicken, filling the air with its succulent aroma. There are tears as the bride's father …

MANUEL STÜBINGER: Clattering dishes, murmur, creamy on the tongue, scent of candles and perfume, candles flicker, stiff suits, elegant dresses, abdominal fullness, hubbub …

Now, your turn. Go.

DAY #10
"WHEN" WRITING

There's plenty of action in "when." One of the more helpful questions you need to ask when you write is, "When is this happening?" Try several answers: "Am I feeling this loss in the spring, when the external world creates an ironic contrast? In the fall, when everything is fading, just like my lost love? In the winter, when I have to protect myself from the chill, like I've been doing since he left? Or summer, when everywhere things are growing in the heat while I shrink emotionally?"

Or, times of day. So many options, so much time available ...

Set a timer and respond to the following prompts for exactly the time allotted. Stop IMMEDIATELY when the timer goes off.

Sight Sound Taste Touch Smell Body Motion

5 minutes: Six in the Morning

CATRINA SEIFFERT: The alarm screamed in my ear jolting me violently from my flying dream. A beautiful relaxing float above the clouds crashed like a plane wreck. My eyes tried desperately to unglue themselves to peer at the neon red lights of my clock radio. My tongue felt (and tasted) like shriveled cardboard and my bloated stomach was the only incentive to venture out of my warm cocoon and onto the ice-cold tiles of the bathroom floor.

CHANELLE DAVIS: Cell phone vibrates on my bedside table, louder and louder, flip it open to stop the noise, warm in winter sheets, eyes tight shut, trying to open, a dim streetlight shines through a crack in the curtain, dark outside, rip open the bedcovers letting the cool air slap my body, bare feet on wooden floors, crouch down search under the bed for a missing gym shoe. Blurry eyes, stretching T-shirt over my head, arm muscles torn and sore, pull my hair back tight into a ponytail and brush my teeth with fresh mint Colgate toothpaste ...

Yikes! Both give a jarring alarm clock experience. Which is more immediate? Why?

Now try it yourself.

10 minutes: First Snowfall

CHANELLE DAVIS: Lift the white mesh curtain, outside snow is drifting through the air, soft and covering the green grass like icing sugar, jump back under the thick sheepskin and press my stomach into the warmth of the bed, walking down Manchester Ave in black furry boots, crunching snow on concrete, breathing in air and frosting my lungs, holding a takeaway Starbucks coffee, cinnamon warms my mouth, snowflakes land on my face and hair, slowly melting, clumps of snow on the carpet disappearing into dark patches, dark streets and church bells echoing, hands snug in mittens in pockets, tight woolen scarf around my neck, stepping carefully around ice, frozen river, skating children bright pink jackets, wobbling, falling, hitting the ice, squirrels darting across the path …

ADAM FARR: Bright, heavy on the eyes, white like a baby rabbit's fur. Everything is coated, padded with an anorak like a huge clumsy boxing glove. I hear dripping from icicles like stalagmite knives and an occasional parachute landing of a pod reentering the garden from the sugary roof.

The cold enters my airways with its purity and my teeth feel large and brittle. My boots labour through layers of crystals, with a sound like an electric bass. I feel myself slipping when the perfect coating gives way and reveals the unexpected dirt beneath. Small petals have been ripped down by the weight of bread-crumb cement, flakes ganging together to pull down branches and enter any vulnerable crack in rocks or clothes. Numb toes flicker trying to regain sensation.

Now it's your turn.

90 seconds: Easter Sunday

JOY GORA: Angelic songs echo high into the arches of the gothic-style church. The smoky scent of incense spirals in the air and walks along the pews—coating worshipers resting on their knees. Wrinkle-free pastel dresses and pressed suits dot the aisle as a halo of sunlight trickles through the kaleidoscope of brilliant colors etched upon the windows. The tart taste of deep red wine lingers on my lips …

CHANELLE DAVIS: Pink flannelette pajamas, smell of Cadbury chocolate in my bedroom, a tower of Easter eggs on my dressing table, little caramel red and blue foil wrapped with polka dots. A big yellow and pink bunny, tear open the foil and sniff it before biting into the ear, bits of chocolate falling down into the hollow centre …

Hot spots: Joy's verbs. Chanelle's chocolate.

Your turn.

DAY #11

"WHEN" WRITING

Today's your last brush with "when." By now I hope you've become pretty good friends. It's a friendship that will last your entire writing life—if you don't ignore it.

Set a timer and respond to the following prompts for exactly the time allotted. Stop IMMEDIATELY when the timer goes off.

Sight Sound Taste Touch Smell Body Motion

5 minutes: Late Evening

CHANELLE DAVIS: Headphones on, swivelling on the computer chair, softly strumming guitar in computer screen light, neighbour upstairs TV muffled through the floor, whisper singing into the microphone, sound of the metronome and buzzing strings from tired sore fingers, move the capo up and down the fretboard, sipping milky Earl Grey tea and eating peanut butter toast to stay awake, outside a lone cricket is singing, roll the seat around on the cold wooden floor trying to get comfortable, guitar nestled into my chest …

ANTHONY CESERI: The sun is dipping down just past the horizon now, coloring the sky with oranges, reds and blues. There's a crisp chill in the air that dances off my skin, and raises up goose bumps. A car passes by on the street to break the silence. Its tires chug along on the asphalt.

The symphony of crickets off in the woods grows louder as the sky darkens. My heart rate at one tick per minute … I feel so calm, my muscles fully relaxed as I stand on the corner against the night sky. I breathe in deep through my nose. I can feel the wind from my breath whooshing up against the sides of the insides of my nostrils.

This prompt seems to have caused a sort of exhalation, a surrender to the calm. Both Chanelle and Anthony get pretty far inside themselves, but I have to confess I'd never felt "the wind from my breath whooshing up against the sides of the insides of my nostrils." Nice.

Now, what have you got?

10 minutes: Loved One's Funeral

DEBORAH QUILTER: I stooped outside the sandstone chapel with sunlight shining down, shriveling inside. The afternoon was a musty grey; filled with blurred empty faces. Muted watercolors trickled down my aching face. My heart was swimming against the current and clogging my every breath. I choked as I tried to speak and darted to avoid compassionate gestures of comfort. I could see white wings and angels as I turned toward the wooden coffin carried by ghostly figures. I felt a steady hand on my shoulder, but no one was there. I stood up in a woozy haze, which flickered in fragments and held onto the pew in front of me in a desperate grip. The heavy cloak of change pressed against my throat as I snatched a shallow gulp of air and battled …

PAUL PENTON: The chapel is small, simple plain walls, the coffin at the end of the room, simply polished wood, no oak. Windows sweep the top of the room, like a classroom, letting in streams of light. The ported strains of the Sandhurst Silver Band he played with for fifteen years hang in the air. Played at the 'Wellington,' had a pool with the smell of rotting fish.

Inside me small earthquakes of confidence fight with rivers of grief.

At the graveside as the coffin sinks below the level of the ground I finally relent with a hot sweep of grief but collect things together. All buried and dead now …

Hot spots: "The heavy cloak of change pressed against my throat … ." "Small earthquakes of confidence."

Now, your turn.

90 seconds: Crossing the Finish Line

CHANELLE DAVIS: Cheeks are burning and flushed red, breathe shallow and panicky heartbeat trying to push my feet to the soft dirt, up the last hill, legs like jelly downhill, sun making my face sweat, T-shirt sweat, feel my chubby stomach bouncing, nausea, feel lump in my throat, tears starting as I see the teachers and parents waiting, pouring orange juice into plastic cups …

KAZ MITCHELL: Trudging through mud on a cross-country run, farmyard fumes from steaming manure filling my nostrils as I gulp in oxygen. My thighs burn as they work to lift boots heavier than lead. The panting of my own breath and the blood sprinting around my brain are all I hear as I see the finish line …

Your turn. Try it out.

There. *Who, what,* and *when* in an ever-enlarging dance. Each an integral partner in creating something riveting, something memorable. One more friend to introduce to the group, starting tomorrow.

DAY #12

"WHERE" WRITING

"Where" can, of course, be anywhere. But it must be somewhere. The Wailing Wall, 42nd Street, the lake cabin, the Grand Canyon, a mountain path, the backseat of the school bus. The opportunities are endless. That's its strength.

"Where" and "when" are a powerful combination, working together to create a scene and situation—a context for "who" and "what" to operate from. They make your writing more palpable, more real. These last three days of the challenge will give you practice locating your characters and the objects around them in various places. You'll be surprised how much muscle your writing will gain from working out with "where."

Set a timer and respond to the following places for exactly the time allotted. Stop IMMEDIATELY when the timer goes off.

5 minutes: A Cliff by the Ocean

NICHOLAS TOZIER: Smell of salt and low tide. Kelp drying on the beach below, dusted with shining flakes of grit and sand. A golden retriever rolling on its back. A boulder near the rocky shore that looks precariously balanced. A child, antlike in the distance, totters into its shade, arm extended to touch the rock's pockmarked side. The boulder shifts. My stomach sinks, mouth opens, legs stir—but the child shrieks a laugh, runs away on wobbly legs, and the rock continues to shift and shift and shift without really moving. Shimmers of heat make everything shimmer and undulate. I lick my lips and they are still salty from a swim ...

CHANELLE DAVIS: Grass is lush green, long and untrimmed as I get closer to the edge. Flax bushes rustling in the wind, Tui bird clinging onto a black stalk, eating the seeds, looking out to blue sea, white-capped waves in the distance, cloudy sky, seagulls hovering like kites, islands in the distance, shadows on horizon, cruise liner slowly moving through the harbour, waves pounding the rocks below, out of sight, lean over the edge and feel dizzy, stumble back and lie down in the grass, sneezing, summer allergies, plane overhead in the sky leaves a long white trail, cars driving up the steep windy hill tires crunching gravel and spinning dust clouds, families posing for photographs with the view, warm clothes, kids chasing each other in circles laughing ...

Sparkling descriptions. They set a wonderful context for action. Put some of your characters in either Nicholas's or Chanelle's scene and watch the colors of the place affect them and how readers feel about them. Give them a thing to hold, like a camera, a pickax, a rifle with a scope, and see how "where" reflects back at them.

Your turn.

10 minutes: Park Bench in the City

CHANELLE DAVIS: Pigeons cooing and flapping around my feet, bobbing heads, diving for bread and scattering when people walk through the square, old cathedral towers up to a bright blue sky, eating fresh strawberry yoghurt ice cream with a wooden stick rough on my tongue, smooth cold sweet ice cream with crunchy strawberry seeds, river water running under the little bridge, ducks taking a ride, punting boats of tourists, busker playing endless solos on guitar through his amplifier, park bench is wooden and curved, fits snug into the shape of my back, avoid the patch of white and green watery bird poo, shoppers bustling past arms heavy with bags, summer sun hot I could be getting burnt, feel it creeping up my neck, undo my hair tie and let out my hair, dig around in my messy handbag for my sunglasses, leave the park bench and head across the square to the sushi shop for salmon and advocado, rip open the plastic container, break the staples, put a whole piece in my mouth …

NELSON BOGART: Blue sky New York April day, park bench with black iron armrests, oak seats worn from the millions of pairs of pants sliding in and out of the now well-worn baskets of brown, wood-grained resting places; pigeons flapping and crying a few feet from this peaceful resting spot, radio-controlled boats gliding silently across the boat pond, tacking jerkily as their captains stride careful along the edge of the pond. Smells of cotton candy, popcorn and deep fry from the little cafe beside the boathouse, strollers and children, gliding by, passed by the roller-bladers, bike racers. The mewing of the pigeons, gulls and laughter. Odd scent of the homeless person who slept on the bench last, the scent of desperation, of no running water. Jazz trumpet, bass and cardboard drum set wafting from the back side of the huge rock formations framing the pond and the statue of Alice in wonderland, so kids crawling all around it while their parents smile as they slide over the brass statue. The percussive interruptions of the thousands of cell phones, chimes and personal ring tones. Armies of park workers in their brown jumpsuits driving electric carts and mowers and the great lawn, home the the greatest frisbee catching dogs, and populated by armies of little kids—Sheesh!!

Great attention to detail. Both give you a panoramic view, but do it by engaging your senses: smells, sounds, sense details like "wooden and curved, fits snug into the shape of my back" and "homeless person who slept on the bench last, the scent of desperation, of no running water."

The better you are at imagining a place, the more activity is possible for your characters because they'll have something to react to. Try it out.

90 seconds: Hotel Bar

JOY GORA: Bunched shoulder-to-shoulder against the slick mahogany bar, Armani suits and long-legged beauties in svelte black dresses litter the night. Martinis and passions. Stirring to jazz jumping in the background. A dim haze of candlelight mingled with the eye-stinging fog of perfume, hairspray and cologne.

MATT K: The bar stool pivots back and forth as my foot swings restlessly over the floor, like a hypnotist's medallion, my eyes scanning the room like the spotlight from a prison tower. Her hips swing with the rhythm of a slithering cobra …

Hot spots: "Armani suits and long-legged beauties in svelte black dresses litter the night" and "eyes scanning the room like the spotlight from a prison tower."

Now, let's hear about your hotel bar.

DAY #13

"WHERE" WRITING

Get your details glasses on. I've heard that's where the devil is. I guess it's fair to say that the devil lives in "where."

Set a timer and respond to the following places for exactly the time allotted. Stop IMMEDIATELY when the timer goes off.

Sight **Sound** **Taste** **Touch** **Smell** **Body** **Motion**

5 minutes: Suburban Swimming Pool

CHANELLE DAVIS: Shrieking kids in colourful togs, my bikini tied up tight around my neck, feel a little bit of my hair caught in it, pulling, sink under the cool water and down to the bottom, sound disappears, open my eyes and feel salt water sting, blurry legs, black lines on the bottom of the pool. Walk across on tiptoes, chin just out of the water, slipping on the tiles, over vents in the bottom exploding air bubbles up my legs, freestyle swim legs kicking and warming my body up, hit in the head with a ball, babies pushed around in floating rings, clapping and smiling, mums trying to keep their hair dry, boys bombing off the side, running and hitting the water, jump out trying to suck my stomach in, walk cool across to the hotpool, jets of water massaging my back, steam ris …

KAZ MITCHELL: Light dances across the water in ripples, the cavernous space filled with a cool sky blue. The choice of easing myself into the icy water wins over plunging in headfirst. The echoing sounds of arms and legs whacking against the surface as dedicated swimmers push themselves from one end to the other then back again, in a hypnotic, trance-like state. Their rhythm works on me like a metronome. Chlorine-scented swimwear get rung out, wrapped up in damp towels then thrown into plastic bags. I crunch hard into a crispy apple as I step out into the grey working day ahead of me.

Hot spots: "… vents in the bottom exploding air bubbles up my legs …"; "I crunch hard into a crispy apple … ."

You try.

10 minutes: The Old Fishing Hole

DEBORAH QUILTER: Trees hunched over the old fishing hole as filtered fins of light hooked through the fluttering leaves. It was tranquil and the water a perfect mirror of clouds and blue satin. When the trees turned green he would head out for weeks at time, tuck his thoughts into his flannel pockets and feel his bare feet on the mud flats where oysters hid among the mangroves. He had rusty old remnants of childhood memories in a squeaking angler's box and hooks and spindles of line collected over the months of ice and sleet, when he'd delicately hook bait from the chest freezer of the local store. He watches the frying pan splatter and spit bubbles of melted butter and toss in fillets …

CHANELLE DAVIS: Oily mackerel in my fingers, browny red flesh, soft and chilled with silver and dotted blue thin skin, scales stick to my hands, push the sharp hook through, pierce the skin and let it dangle off the wharf, flick the bailer arm on my reel and let the nylon spool off, sinking down into the green-blue water, look over the wooden edge, big wooden pylons covered in green slime and barnacles, little bits of sea lettuce floating on the top, tiny spotties darting around in groups, feel the tugging on my rod and quickly wind it up, little fish jiggling on my hook, flapping in the wind, carefully hold him in my palm, he wriggles as I force the hook free and throw him into mum's red laundry bucket, he swims round in circles with the others, one dead and white belly up on the surface. Seagulls stalking, looking for scraps of bait, squawking and boat engines humming, diesel fumes cloud the air, my feet are warm in gumboots, old grey track pants. Bits of fish on my pants where I wiped my hands clean, fish under my nails, salty and dry, open the flask of steaming milo and pour into the flimsy plastic cup. Blow it cool before sipping, careful not to trip in the cracks of the wharf, chicken and relish sandwiches on white bread, smell like plastic wrap, dry on the corners, buttery and filling …

Hot spots: "Trees hunched over the old fishing hole as filtered fins of light hooked through the fluttering leaves." "Tuck his thoughts into his flannel pockets."

I feel like I've been fishing after reading Chanelle's piece.

Try Deborah's piece in present tense. Then translate it into first person, then second person.

Now write about your own fishing hole.

90 seconds: Under an Umbrella

PAUL PENTON: Drops rush by, making a wet phutting sound on the synthetic cover. The smell of rain coming in from the sea, the smell of the tar unleashing trapped dirt and chemicals and road grit. The taste of the rain in the air, clean fresh. Mist trying to fly sideways swiping my face …

MATT K: Rain spatters the umbrella that barely covers our heads as we crouch next to each other by the wall of the old hotel, looking out over the deserted beach stretching like an empty highway. We cower like two rabbits shivering underneath a rock as we listen to the small pellets of angry water pounding on the nylon, like rubber bullets against a shield. It's the sound of a ruined vacation.

Nice details in both of these: "a wet phutting sound," "the smell of the tar unleashing trapped dirt," and "small pellets of angry water pounding on the nylon." They really take the reader there.

Now, you try.

DAY #14

"WHERE" WRITING

Wow! The final day of this challenge. Almost there …

Here we go!

Set a timer and respond to the following places for exactly the time allotted. Stop IMMEDIATELY when the timer goes off.

Sight **Sound** **Taste** **Touch** **Smell** **Body** **Motion**

5 minutes: On the City Bus

PAUL PENTON: My chair becomes a massage-o-matic as I sit high over the rear wheels. The lights change and the driver stamps on the pedal, the motor reaches for a soprano 'C' and we're moving again. The brakes need changing, every new stop it's the scree of complaint from just under me. Hungry now, stomach punches me for food, waiting to get a premade bacon and egg—the yolks explode and mix with the smoky bacon and the way the toast sandpapers my tongue. This morning, cold fingers were brushing my face; winter is almost here: I emerged from the house to a hint of cloud as I breathed. So the bus jumps and jives over the last tram tracks and swings its disco dance around traffic lights, depositing me on the corner near the gallery. The driver stamps again and the engine complains its way down Southbank Boulevard …

KAZ MITCHELL: A freezing wind hurtles off the Firth of Forth as I wait for the No. 17 into Edinburgh. I stamp my feet, rub my hands, pace up-and-down the worn pavement to warm my blood. Finally, I hear the chugging of its engine before I see its maroon skin ease into sight and pull up like a tired and unwilling beast of burden. I screw up my nose at the leaking petrol smell from its hulk, but quickly climb up to the top deck. I admire the view of the estuary, stretching out like a tongue searching for a salty kiss.

Paul's metaphors and Kaz's similes are wonderful. And both pieces are so full of energy. More on metaphor and simile in the next challenge. For now, go back and pick them out.

Your turn.

10 minutes: Wedding in an Old Church

DEBORAH QUILTER: The door is rickety and splinters catch in my palm as I push it wide open. The floorboards creak and puff of dust lassoes my creeping ballet slippers. It's perfect, this ramshackle gem, in the leafy woods. I press my eyes closed to see pretty lights made out of paper roses and the scent of pine and wonder brushing by. I can hear the band playing my favorite songs from days when I was too small to see up over the window ledge. I peer down at my finger to a sparkle, and smile. I hold the wooden bench soon to be wrapped in tightened vines and step into a stream of violet light and shadows. The soft breeze of certainty whistles …

KAZ MITCHELL: It's cool inside the church, and the light is gentle as it streams through stained glass. Images of Christ hush the expectant crowd, controlling their small talk to mere mumbles. Someone passes around polo mints to suck while they wait. Children blow steam from their mouths into the cold air, tired of sitting on hard wooden pews next to old aunts in floral dresses and floppy hats. The rising swell of the organ fills the space and silences the whispering. Heads turn to the bride marching down the aisle, her footsteps clipped against the hard, grey stone, a trail of Nina Ricci following her like a puppy. Her nerves jump right out of her skin as she approaches the man standing stiff as a sheet left out to dry in the frost. He, on the other hand, can feel the warmth come seeping back to him knowing she's finally arrived.

See how active these are? Both are written in first-person present tense. They involve multiple senses and use metaphor and simile: "puff of dust lassoes my creeping ballet slippers," "the man standing stiff as a sheet left out to dry in the frost."

"Where" is a wonderful tool. Once you decide the place, the rest of your writing can wrap around it or evolve from it. That's why it's useful to imagine a place when you write, whether or not you actually talk about it. "Where" organizes action.

Abstract, generic writing usually lacks the grounding power of "where."

Your turn.

90 seconds: Canoe on the River

CHRIS COWAN: With its yoke on my shoulders, I stumble under the weight of the canoe. Flipping it into the water, we board, and I kneel in the stern. I use a slow J stroke, noticing the little whirlpools in lapping rhythm. My partner scans for telltale Vs, marking rocks waiting in ambush …

KAZ MITCHELL: Putting my weight into it, I feel every muscle in my arm ache as I glide through calm, clear waters. A slapping sound, as the oars hit the water, echoes around me. Ducks, in a flurry of panic and noise, get out of the way. I slide past tall, elegant gum trees, pouring out their medicinal scent like I pour out my sweat.

Nice. This canoe trip takes you to the next challenge. Ready to pour out your sweat where rocks wait in ambush? Try it.

Congratulations on finishing your first challenge!

Writing from the senses is such a powerful tool because of the way it involves the readers' own sense memories, making the world you create *their* world—it's full of *their* stuff! So the better you get at sense-bound writing, the more effectively you can touch others, not to mention how stimulating and nourishing it is to your own writing process.

I hope you've been doing this challenge with partners. Doing so not only keeps you on point, it's a great way to get to know each other. People do it at home, in professional writers' rooms, in classrooms, centers for kids at risk, and I've even heard of folks using it as an icebreaker at dinner parties: "It changes the level of conversation completely—and for the better!"

The second challenge is looming, and you can dive right in if you'd like. But it might be good to take a few days, or even a few weeks, off. Take the time to digest what you've done and make it part of your bloodstream.

Of course, nobody is stopping you from continuing object writing on your own. Or you might go to www.objectwriting.com for the daily prompt there.

Whenever you start the second challenge, just make sure you *do* start it. It'll change the way you write. I promise.

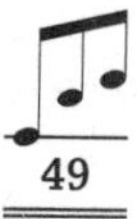

CHALLENGE #2

METAPHOR

Metaphors have a way of holding the most truth in the least space.

—ORSON SCOTT CARD

Welcome to Challenge #2. After what you've just done, writing from your senses on *who, what, where,* and *when,* this challenge is a natural follow-up. All those specifics you learned to wade into can be even more interesting if they're not only what they *are,* but become more than they are—they can transform or be transformed if they are seen through the lens of another idea. Added weight. Added meaning.

A metaphor is a collision between ideas, one idea crunched into another—which is itself a metaphor: Metaphors aren't really collisions, unless you think of ideas as cars, and some of them running into each other, colliding. Then you can think about *ideas* in car terms.

Think of a word like *collision* as establishing a tone center, like a musical key. Some notes belong fully with it. Some have a bit of tension in the relationship, but still belong to the family. These are called "diatonic to" (or related to) the idea. Two ideas collide when they are in different keys, different families, like *idea* and *collision*. A third thing emerges: a chord that contains them both. A metaphor.

So now you start thinking about the things cars do, always looking for things that they could have in common with an *idea*.

An idea might be:

Broken down along the roadside (flat tire?)
Ticketed for speeding
Taking the scenic route
Parked in the garage

C'mon, add some of your own. I'll wait.

People see and use metaphor every day. It's a truly human activity—seeing one thing as though it were something else—an idea as a car, for example. When you say, "Don't forget to stop and smell the roses," you are using metaphor. Stopping to smell a rose is an act— it's just a moment taken to stimulate your olfactory nerve. But it is used to mean, "Slow down and enjoy yourself. Pay attention to the beauty around you." Smelling the roses could be cooking a nice dinner, window shopping, holding hands ... .

Take a look at types of metaphors, then you can launch into making them. Don't let the grammatical classifications put you off. It's easy stuff, really, and very useful, since we all use nouns, verbs, and adjectives pretty regularly.

TYPES OF METAPHOR

Expressed Identity—asserts an identity between two **nouns**, e.g., *fear* is a *shadow; a cloud* is a *sailing ship*. Expressed identity comes in three forms:

"x is y" (fear is a shadow)
"The y of x" (the shadow of fear)
"x's y" (fear's shadow)

EXERCISE: Run each of these through all three forms:

wind = yelping dog
wind = river
wind = highway

Now come up with a few of your own and run them through all three forms. You might even extend them into longer versions, e.g., clouds are sailing ships on rivers of wind.

Qualifying Metaphor—adjectives qualify nouns; adverbs qualify verbs. Friction within these relationships creates metaphor, e.g., hasty clouds; to sing blindly.

Verbal Metaphor—formed by conflict between the verb and its subject and/or object, e.g., clouds sail; he tortured his clutch; frost gobbles summer down.

Aristotle said that the ability to see one thing as another is the only truly creative human act. Most people have the creative spark to make metaphors, they just need to train and direct their energy properly. Look at this metaphor from Shelley's *Ode to the West Wind*: "A heavy weight of hours has chained and bowed/One too like thee ..."

Hours are links of a chain, accumulating weight and bending the old man's back lower and lower as each new hour is added. An interesting way to look at old age ...

Great metaphors seem to come in a flare of inspiration—there is a moment of light and heat, and suddenly the writer sees the old man bent over, dragging a load of invisible hour-chains. But even if great metaphors come from inspiration, you can certainly prepare yourself for their flaring. Here are some exercises to train your vision; to help you learn to look in the hot places; to help you nurture a spark that can erupt into something bright and wonderful. Have fun.

★ ★ ★ ★ ★

DAY #1

ADJECTIVE-NOUN COLLISIONS

Okay, here you go. You'll start with some straightforward exercises that collide grammatical types, nouns with adjectives, nouns with verbs, even nouns with nouns. The goal is to take these arbitrary collisions and explore the ideas these combinations suggest.

You'll start with adjectives and nouns. Today you'll have ten prompts, each requiring a sentence or short paragraph and then a ninety-second piece of object writing. A total of fifteen minutes, not counting the thinking and the sentences. Should be easy, eh?

First, you have to sit and think about the collision; try to supply a landscape to make it make sense. That takes a bit of time at first, but you'll get faster as you go.

Once you've made sense of the collision, timed object writing on it will allow you to explore its facets quickly. So you'll do a ninety-second piece of object writing using the collision as a prompt.

Here are the lists:

ADJECTIVES	NOUNS
Lonely	Moonlight
Blackened	Funeral
Fallen	Carburetor
Smooth	Autumn
Fevered	Handkerchief

Take the first adjective in its list and shove it up against the first noun in the noun list. You get "lonely moonlight." Where does it take you? Maybe ...

Lonely Moonlight

SUSAN CATTANEO: Daylight hurried away, leaving lonely moonlight to console the solitary oak tree that wept autumn leaves.

90 seconds: *Rickety house stands at attention, its dormers like epaulets on shingle shoulders, keeping vigil over the park. Crumpled up newspapers skip and twirl like batons near the grate at the curb. Silence descends like a hawk. The tart tang of skunk pulls at my nose.*

BEN ROMANS: The moonlight is a lonely wallflower on the waves, waiting for another beam to offer its hand, to ask it to waltz.

90 seconds: *The lonely moonlight listens to the waves, as it pierces the ocean like a needle on vinyl. It plays like a muted trumpet. Boats are a recipe of dust ...*

You'll be seeing a lot of Susan. She's pretty good at this. She took words that belong to *lonely*, like *forsaken* and, instead of people forsaking each other, "Daylight hurried away, leaving lonely moonlight ... ." Personification. Simple. And effective.

And Ben has the moonlight at a school dance ...

Susan's object writing reeks of isolation. She probably got to the house from the oak tree in her sentence. And Ben's picture of moonlight listening is exciting, and then to move from listening to music? Nice.

Your object writing should use *lonely moonlight* as its prompt, but note how far afield you can go. Anywhere is possible. You just get there through lonely moonlight's gate. Go ahead. Give it a shot.

Blackened Funeral

CHANELLE DAVIS: It was a blackened funeral, with hundreds of umbrellas sheltering the people from a typical wet November afternoon as they listened to a prayer being read over the loud speaker ...

Long black woolen coats buttoned high and scarves, purple wrapped tight around necks, ushers and rows and rows of blackened people, running mascara down porcelain cheeks, red scarlet lips splash colour like a flick of paint from a brush ...

SUSAN CATTANEO: Hot August sun broils the asphalt, and the limousines line up grill to bumper, charcoal briquettes at a blackened funeral.

The widow bends over the open grave and drops a white rose into the darkened mouth of earth. Mourners holding tissues close, keen quietly as the dark casket's holy ...

You'll be seeing a lot more of Chanelle, too. Note how both she and Susan litter their writing with black—umbrellas, coats, mascara, asphault, charcoal briquettes, and "the darkened mouth of earth."

Now, you try.

Fallen Carburetor

GREG BECKER: After 43 years of smoking his Marlboro Reds, he grabs his chest in his final moments as his fallen carburetor coughs and chokes out its final breath.

Deep within his chest the echoes of laughter and a strong young voice bounce off the metallic tar-stained fallen carburetor that once was a pink lung—the carburetor that, in his younger days could take a breath large enough to throw a touchdown pass or blow out the candles on a cake, now just sat rusted within him.

SUSAN CATTANEO: The preacher's old station wagon preached a sermon of exhaust as it rumbled downtown, its fallen carburetor backfiring rhetoric.

Bibles rise precariously like stairs in the passenger seat, the radio tuned to Sunday's sermon blasts hymn through scratchy speakers, tight white suspenders and a starched white shirt, wedding ring suffocating the puffy left ring finger …

Pretty interesting: Greg sees a lung as a carburetor, coughing and choking—verbs that work with either lungs or carburetors. And Susan turns the preacher into a car "backfiring rhetoric."

Your turn.

Smooth Autumn

ANNE HALVORSEN: School bells announce the autumn smooth with old comforts.

Scent of newly sharp pencils, pristine erasers, top zip cases fitting neatly on notebook rings, snaps of binders pinching fingers as they close over endless white circles licked and placed, reinforcing holes already ripped …

CHANELLE DAVIS: This was a smooth autumn, yellow leaves slick and dripping with fresh rain, sticking to my boots. The river was swollen and I watched the ducks gliding in pairs, every now and again a quack breaking the misty silence.

Layers of leaves, sweet rotting smell, squirrels running with wet feet, licking wet fur, cloudy sky, hidden sun, warm hands around a takeaway Starbucks cup, standing in the park rain falling from trees, on my forehead, still air, shiny concrete, washed away chalk hopscotch game, empty playground...

Hot spots: "School bells announce..."; "yellow leaves slick and dripping with fresh rain."

Now, your turn.

Fevered Handkerchief

GREG BECKER: After several days of the flu he crawls out of bed no more than a fevered handkerchief with pillow imprints wrinkled into his cheeks.

Fevered handkerchief is a grumpy rumplestiltskin rag tossed aside after cooling off a sweaty brow, the linen sponge filled with sickness and sweat, thirsty for a cool breeze to dry off its hard night's work. It lays exhausted in its own pile of success.

IAN HENCHY: The fevered handkerchief sprinted from the man's weathered hands to his nose, just in time to catch the volcanic sneeze and keep the bacteria-ridden lava from spewing about the room.

The virgin-white handkerchief served as his trusty sidekick throughout cold and flu season. It sat, perched like a parrot in the breast pocket of his business blazer for whenever it was needed. It still smelled factory fresh, a slightly abrasive dry-clean smell with soft undertones.

Pretty interesting handkerchiefs, eh?

Now write your own version.

Five down, five to go. The words have been mixed up a bit, and you'll do the same thing for each new adjective/noun combination., Again, write a sentence, then a ninety-second piece for each collision, using it as the prompt.

ADJECTIVES	NOUNS
Lonely	Handkerchief
Blackened	Autumn
Fallen	Funeral

Smooth	Moonlight
Fevered	Carburetor

Lonely Handkerchief

JESS MEIDER: An angel flew from the fingers of a hand in a sin-red BMW convertible, onto the desert ashphalt. A long highway snaking from horizon to horizon, as the lonely handkerchief lies crumpled on the ground, weeping for its circumstance.

Sitting decoratively in the man's breast pocket, the handkerchief listens to the conversations intently, waiting for some pretty eyes to press into its neatly pressed corner from laughing so hard that the tears come bubbling up, like the laughter from her sensual belly.

GREG BECKER: The gowns and tuxedos had all gone home, tossing him aside for the evening, nothing but a lonely handkerchief crumpling into himself, clutching his near empty glass.

Lonely handkerchief sits crumpled at the bottom of a tuxedo breast jacket pocket; folds of origami crisscross its Picasso face. Smooth silk speaks a different language of touch. No one spoke tonight.

I love the "sin-red BMW," and the way Jess personifies the handkerchief. Personification—attributing human characteristics to nonhuman things—is just one of the many ways to make a metaphor. Just another way to create collisions.

It's hard to tell in Greg's sentence whether he's talking about a person or a piece of cloth. I like when that happens: Call it "productive ambiguity," having at least two meanings, and both work in the context. You'll find that productive ambiguity lies at the heart of metaphor.

Now, you try.

Blackened Autumn

ANNE HALVORSEN: The fire left a blackened autumn, wild flames visible across the great bay.

Flames stripped the green, ate the flower and vegetable gardens one by one, leapt to gold and red leaves then sucked the trees in its mouth and skipped across the roofs gobbling houses leaving grey looming fireplaces, misshapen unrecognizable pieces of home, then, a swing frame in the sodden yard ...

CHANELLE DAVIS: The children couldn't see any of the usual bright red or orange leaves. The autumn had been blackened by bushfires that turned red and gold leaves to ash.

Charcoal trees, stumps, dusty gray ash flakes landing on my coat, floating on raindrops, dark threatening clouds, rumbling thunder ...

Of course, the fires in both pieces blacken things, not the season. So to say that the fire blackened *autumn* is, like all metaphor, literally false. In fact, if the combination could be true, e.g., *blackened handkerchief*, then it's not a metaphor. Again, metaphors are always literally false. That's what makes them interesting.

Your turn.

Fallen Funeral

IAN HENCHY: Rather than being a celebration of life, it was a fallen funeral—victim to the cause of death: a suicide.

The surprised casket remained closed, hiding the face that the parents were now so ashamed to display. No red roses surrounded the casket, no floral arrangements. The family seeping silent resentment.

ANNE HALVORSEN: It was to be an event, a gathering, instead it was a fallen funeral, such a failure as these things go.

She wrapped the bird in layers of Easter-colored tissue and plastic grass, placed him gently in the shoebox from mother's closet, and walked grandly to the tall oak, the retriever striding softly at her side ...

Ian's take on the funeral, which could have been a celebration, has descended into something else. Anne gives a fallen bird a funeral. Nice.

Now, your turn.

Smooth Moonlight

BONNIE HAYES: The smooth moonlight pours like thick cream through the window.

Spilling across my floor. Silken, undulating—I want to get out of bed and go stand in it, dance in it, let it fall in folds across my skin, feel it on my hair …

BEN ROMANS: The moonlight carved into the landscape, stroking the hills as smooth as a brush.

The smooth moonlight sunk into the desert ahead. The crickets applauded the shadows' ballet on the sand. The rest of the sky was envious of the feast below …

Hot spots: "smooth moonlight pours like thick cream" and "stroking the hills as smooth as a brush."

Your turn.

Fevered Carburetor

BLEU: The carburetor was fevered, sputtering the car to life like a half-drowned man coughing up water.

… sputtering to a halt … grinding … sweating … oil—enough fumes to get you high … speed–demon … faster … harder … clutching, the clutch, with bare feet … pushing the pedal so far beyond (through) the vinyl car-mat the asphalt is giving you a manicure … sick … with smoke … bad emissions …

SUSAN CATTANEO: On the off ramp, halfway between Phoenix and Flagstaff, the fevered carburetor fainted, giving a huge steam-filled sigh.

Tires sag into the blacktop and the heat shimmers on the horizon. The buzz-saw sound of cicadas and the starched feeling in my throat, smell of mesquite and the starched white sun …

Now, your turn.

Whew! Quite an introduction to this challenge. The work you've done today has put you on a road that will take your writing places it hasn't likely been too regularly. These metaphor exercises will change the way you look at the world. You'll see more on the vertical—things stacking on top of each other—rather than horizontally. Things in a line will become only what they are.

Rest now. Another day is coming.

DAY #2

FINDING NOUNS FROM ADJECTIVES

Yesterday I gave you the combinations and asked you to explore them. Today, I'll give you the adjectives, leaving it up to you to find nouns to crunch up against them. Don't grab just anything; take your time and look for provocative, productive collisions.

If you need a nudge finding nouns, or any grammatical type for that matter, *Roget's International Thesaurus*, the nondictionary-style thesaurus, is a good friend. It's a great place to hunt, and it corrals nouns, verbs, adjectives, and adverbs into their own separate pens.

As you did yesterday, write a sentence or short paragraph for each collision. Then do a ninety-second piece of object writing for each collision, using it as the object.

Angry ___________

ANDREA STOLPE

Angry *taxes*: I drove my pencil through the tangle of unsure numbers and stale questions, trying to make some sense of my angry taxes.

Snap, another graphite stick bites the dust. Numbers blur, questions stare me down like a buffalo on the plains of North Dakota, my eyes slurring words as my nightlight pops and clicks—tiny fruit flies flitting to their death around April 15th.

KEPPIE COUTTS

Angry *umbrella*: My angry umbrella flails and pops its arms inside out and refuses to budge back into shape.

The brooding clouds quickly take on a violent edge, turning a nasty shade of purple and brown, a big swelling bruise in the sky. Thick hot droplets spit as I pop my umbrella, but the wind carries the rain at impossibly aggressive angles.

Of course, the trick here is to remember that metaphor is always literally false. Don't pick something that can be literally angry, like people or bees. Those wouldn't be metaphors. They'd just be angry people and angry bees. Both Andrea and Keppie chose nouns that don't belong to *angry*'s family.

Now, you try.

Boastful ___________

SUSAN CATTANEO

Boastful *flag*: Buoyed by the cheering whistle of the wind, the boastful flag puffed out its chest revealing the proud white, red and blue.

Starched blue uniforms lined up like pencils, the glare of the tuba and trumpet, summer popsicles melting down children's chins, the creak and complaining of the plaid lawn chair as its straps are stretched …

ANDREA STOLPE

Boastful *hallway*: Upon entering through massive doors of intimidation we were ushered down a boastful hallway.

White. Shiny and white. Sour sweet smell of disinfectant sleeked across smooth granite floors. Massive chandelier glittery and offensive, hanging like a memorial of plucked chickens strung from their bony wrinkled feet.

Again, both Susan and Andrea chose nouns that are nondiatonic to *boastful*. That's why they collide.

Your turn.

Careful____________

BONNIE

Careful *light*: A careful ray of light slinks into the room sideways.

Not through the window but through the crack under the door. With as little fanfare as possible, it edges up my face to a similar crack in my eyelid, and very gently slips into my consciousness. I'd rather keep this reckless darkness behind my eyes.

SUSAN CATTANEO

Careful *sunrise*: The careful sunrise stepped gently over the mountain's fragile shoulders.

Dipping an orange velvet slipper into the morning, the sunrise twirls her colorful skirts in the spring air, her voice is the melody of a robin's trill, a child's laugh on a carousel …

Interesting what these collisions can spawn. I'd never thought of a mountain as having fragile shoulders before. Nor of light *slinking*. Once you introduce *careful*'s family to *sunrise*'s family, or *light*'s family, all sorts of couplings and conversations can happen.

Your turn.

Dark ____________

SUSAN CATTANEO

Dark *lie*: Our love was a white sheet blowing on a summer clothesline and his dark lie was a stain that would never come clean.

Wind playing hide-and-seek in the cornfields, the distant drone of a tractor, hard rough hands, red and blotchy, plunge into the cold water, pulling the wet clothes out and dragging them across the washboard …

JESS MEIDER

Dark *static*: Dark static hung low and humming in the shady ancient temple.

Too far after midnight, I drive into the spotlight cast ten feet ahead, never quite arriving, eyes deliberately dart like the dot above karaoke lyrics, the words unclear, fuzzy.

Fingers twist the knob, voices mixed with notes scramble in and out like some far away alter reality. Then blaring audio AM radio fuzz jolts me out of a trance—a dark static, frightening and full of voices, intimidating like large machinery, too much like a box of ghosts that I would rather not open.

Remember, dark *eyes* could be literally true, and thus isn't a metaphor. They join together rather than colliding. Dark *thoughts*, though a cliché, is a metaphor. It's literally false.

Your turn.

Enthusiastic ___________

CHANELLE DAVIS

Enthusiastic *balloons*: I chase the bunch of enthusiastic balloons as they scramble across the lawn and glide over the neatly clipped hedge, floating further and further into the summer sky …

Rainbow colours, rubber stretched tight, full of helium, white ribbons trailing after them, bouncing trying to break free, hot breeze …

SUSAN CATTANEO

Enthusiastic *flip-flops*: The Jersey shore boardwalk was filled with the chatter of enthusiastic flip-flops.

Cut-off jeans and a transistor radio, hair teased high like a dark tornado, eyes black and blue with mascara and eye shadow. Her accent sneers out of pink lips, tattoos like veins around her delicate wrists.

I love the picture of balloons scrambling across the lawn.

Susan's back in "who" writing in her ninety seconds. Thinking of flip-flops chattering turns them into mouths. Neat.

Give it a try.

Good for you. You've taken an important step, looking for one of the elements in the collision. It makes you think up a lot of possibilities before you get one that vibrates. Looking for the noun from the quality (adjective) is a pretty interesting search. Another wrinkle coming tomorrow.

DAY #3

FINDING ADJECTIVES FROM NOUNS

Yesterday I gave you an adjective and asked you to look for a colliding noun. Today, the process is reversed: I'll give you the noun, and you try to find a colliding adjective.

Again, don't just grab anything; take your time and look for provocative, productive combinations.

As usual, write a sentence or short paragraph that makes sense of the combination. Then do a ninety-second piece of object writing for each collision, using it as the object.

____________ Furnace

KRISTIN CIFELLI

***Hungry* furnace:** The hungry furnace ran nonstop through the dead of winter, consuming natural gas like a marathon runner devours power bars.

Eating up coal, and keeping us warm … running, running, running—tired and running making its own heat in the cold, damp basement, surrounded by cobwebs and empty boxes … sparks flying, creaking stairs down to the basement, winter's best friend …

SUSAN CATTANEO

***Wheezing* furnace:** The silence in my grandfather's basement was interrupted by the coughs and sputters of the wheezing furnace, lungs full of stale hot air …

Train tracks like scars on the surface of the ping-pong table, dust motes floating through the weak light coming in from the basement transom window, spiders lying in wait in webbed corners, rusty tools and the dented wooden surface, smell of mothballs and old socks …

What does a furnace do? Okay, it consumes energy, it blows hot air. What else consumes energy? People? People consume energy when they're hungry. Aha! Hungry furnace. What else blows hot air—

exhales? Human beings do. When humans are old and worn, their lungs may not be that great. Aha! Wheezing furnace.

Your turn.

____________ Midnight

JESS MEIDER

***Angular* midnight:** Angular midnight interjecting, never protesting; time pours itself into this metallic night, reflections from every surface …

Beijing midnight is angular, edges and sides multiplied as in a dark diamond. Food-stands with miniature stools around flip-up tables, meat on sticks fry over red and black coals, by a Uighur man in a white boxy fitted hat. Disco kids with zany silver and gold flash! Tiny giggles wearing tiny skirts, eyes dilated in techno beats, just dipping out and then dipping back in. A work horse hitched to a cart babbles along past it all, unnoticed, back to his peasant village in a wrinkled mountain.

ANNE HALVORSEN

***Sable* midnight:** Sable midnight, a velour pullover for the hills.

Dreams of the rusted steel mills and factories once running night and day. Memories of the lake's miles-long twinkling lights, all steam and smoke at daylight, leaving the sky forever tinted. Men walk with their high-top lunchboxes to welcome work, not privy to black waves hitting sand …

Hot spots: "his peasant village in a wrinkled mountain," "velour pullover for the hills."

Your turn.

____________ Cottage

ANDREA STOLPE

***Trembling* cottage:** The overgrowth of the forest twined its needy vines around the trembling cottage, squeezing rafter from roof and distorting every right angle.

We arrived with the last few rays of an October afternoon. The cabin looked less like a romantic getaway than a case for backwoods welfare. I imagined that if I exhaled too intensely the whole structure might collapse. But then, perhaps I was the wolf and you the pig, and this was just our way ...

SUSAN CATTANEO

***Uptight* cottage:** A perfectly manicured lawn, perky white fence and a prim red mailbox separated the uptight cottage from the slovenly condo complex that squatted next door ...

Music blares out of car stereo speakers, the old man hikes up his trousers and leans down to prune the roses that line his driveway, he scowls at the children running like sprites through the open fire hydrant ...

Andrea draws her adjective, *trembling*, from the verb, to tremble. Adjectives created in this sort of way, by adding *ing* or *ed* to the verb, are called *participles*. Since verbs are the strongest element in language, using them to create adjectives makes for a more potent modifier.

"The slovenly condo complex that squatted next door ... ." Yum.

Now, you try.

____________ Hope

ANDREA STOLPE

***Fragile* hope:** Her stance emanates a fragile hope, shoulders sloping and an anxious trembling in her fingers as she petitions the school board for more money.

I feel that surge of anxiety as I stand here in my navy heels and black hose. I know I should have dressed in the natural light of the bedroom rather than fumbling through my top dresser drawer in the dim light of the bedside reading lamp.

SUSAN CATTANEO

***Sharp* hope:** Waiting for him to call, she felt the sharp hope pierce her heart every time the phone rang.

A number scrawled on a beer-soaked napkin, regret burns like a cigarette, tousled sheets on the empty bed, high-heeled shoes tossed on the couch, morning breath and mascara running down ...

Hope is one of those abstract nouns. *Trust, love,* etc., all need something specific to ground them. Both Andrea and Susan give us adjectives with enough spunk to crunch up against an ocean liner like *hope*.

Your turn.

____________ Ghost

SUSAN CATTANEO

***Lazy* ghost:** The loose shutter on the house swung back and forth halfheartedly, pushed by the languid hand of a lazy ghost.

Porch sagging like an old woman's stockings, grass brown and yellow in patches, the old light blue Monte Carlo, tires as flat as deflated old balloons, swallows pitch and yaw like tiny black kites in and out of the eaves …

ANDREA STOLPE

***Porcelain* ghost:** Her mother's support was only a porcelain ghost, kept out of reach on a pedestal and debated whether to exist at all.

My grandmother's dresser was a sacred place. Old photographs beaten by changing seasons stood in a matronly fashion atop a varnished oak surface. Mothballs and century-old perfume leached into every pore of the wood, every unmentionable underclothing hidden within those drawers. I wondered what people of that generation tucked under their pile of socks …

These both work, but note that a ghost might be realistically deemed lazy as opposed to active. Not quite a collision. Of course, that ghosts don't exist helps. They don't, right?

Rather than a collision of the two terms, *porcelain ghost* seems to refer to a bust or picture of a dead grandfather. Nice overtones, though it feels somewhere between metaphor and euphemism.

Since *ghost* can have human qualities, try unhuman qualities like *brittle* or *wrinkled*. C'mon, you can do it.

DAY #4

NOUN-VERB COLLISIONS

Verbs. You've already learned something about them. They're the most potent force in language. Nouns are inert. They sit there. Adjectives pile on top of them and sit there. Verbs electrify them, propel them, launch them into action. The difference between average and great writing: verbs.

Today you'll create collisions between verbs and nouns. As on day 1, I'll give you two lists: a list of nouns and a list of verbs. It'll be up to you to make something of the collision.

NOUNS	VERBS
Moonlight	Tumble
Funeral	Exhale
Carburetor	Sing
Autumn	Remembers
Handkerchief	Plead

For each noun/verb combination, write a sentence or short paragraph expanding on the association. Of course, adjust the verb's number and tense to suit the noun and the context.

Then do a ninety-second piece of object writing for each combination, using it as the prompt.

Moonlight Tumbles

LEORA SALO: Moonlight tumbles through the lace curtains weaving webs on your skin, my fingers as spiders. I like the way your skin crawls under my touch.

Where we once wove the sheets in tapestry of our life together, the moonlight now is just a stubborn child that tumbles into my bed and will not leave me alone.

JAMES MERENDA: Moonlight tumbles into the more hidden nooks of the city.

Rolling under the traffic of the clouds, doggedly making its way, twice-reflected, onto the street, weary from its work, it is either romantic, or dying. Perhaps both.

You can feel the collision between nouns and verbs. A verb like *tumble* belongs to a pretty active family, which suggests Lia's "stubborn child." Note James's additional metaphor "the traffic of the clouds." Nice.

Now, you try.

Funeral Exhales

CHANELLE DAVIS: The tsunami exhaled a funeral onto the white beach, finally withdrawing to the deep ocean it was born from.

Bodies laying still, twisted like pretzels, some look like they're sleeping, piles of broken buildings like matchsticks, beached ships, roads ripped apart, black wave overtaking the land ...

ANDREA STOLPE: The funeral exhaled the stench of greedy family members waiting to collect on the will.

I couldn't look at the priest so I studied the bare dirt with sprigs of destitute grass lurching around our shined shoes and morose suit pants. I could feel the eyes digging into my back, my brother's wife releasing her resentment like an IV drip over twenty years of knowing and hating me ...

Note in Chanelle's response that the noun *funeral* comes after the verb as a direct object, with another noun, *tsunami,* providing the subject. That's the beauty of noun/verb collisions: The noun can serve either as subject or direct object.

"Stench" belongs to *exhale*'s tone center, while "greedy family members" is in a different key, creating the collision. Nice.

Your turn.

Carburetor Sings

CHANELLE DAVIS: The carburetor sings as they flee down the open desert highway ...

High-pitched drone, revving engine, quickly changing the clutch, high speed, see the needle pass 100, leather seat burning hot on my thigh, arm tanning on the window and hair streaming behind me, open my mouth and let the rushing air dry out my saliva …

JESS MEIDER: the mechanic "whisperer" turns the motor, it raps and bumps in a strange ghetto rhythm while the fans squeal in delight and the carburetor sings a wavering, sweet sick melody …

Home beacon, I can see it, little light calling my eyes to its tiny star calling from the mountains. The gas big E pointer finger red and thin, a babbling exhausted metal body chugging as though it will only take a few more breaths, as the carburetor sings a eulogy, swollen and sullen.

So many possibilities here. So many kinds of songs. And in the mouth of a carburetor …

You give it a try.

Autumn Remembers

CHANELLE DAVIS: Autumn remembers you dancing in its fallen leaves and wonders where you have gone.

Raking leaves into a pile under the oak tree, falling in it, waist deep, buried, brown and crinkly they scratch my skin and get in my mouth, spit them out, chasing you round and round the pile till we're dizzy and fall over …

SUSAN CATTANEO: Every year, autumn opens its scrapbook and remembers the color of decay, turning the page of each yellowed leaf and fondly tracing the sky with bare finger branches …

Leaves kicked up by a childish wind, smoke curling lazily out the brick chimneys, pulling the wool jacket in closer, a ghost of breath comes out of open lips in the morning …

This prompt personifies autumn. It's up to you to find the memories. If, on the other hand, *autumn* is the direct object of *remembers*, you'll look for a collision using the form "___________ remembers autumn." Just make sure the noun you choose doesn't actually have the ability to remember.

Now, give it a try.

Handkerchief Pleads

ANDREA STOLPE: My handkerchief pleaded for allergy season to pass as I released an army of pollen-induced explosions into the worn cotton weave.

I remember my dad's handkerchiefs, soft from months or even years of washing and the faint powdery scent of the dryer sheet tumbling and caressing it in the washer. Like his T-shirts, the fabric would gradually thin until the tan of his skin would lend a darker hue to the white as he wore it.

SUSAN CATTANEO: Balled up in the old man's pocket, the wrinkled handkerchief pleaded for a good ironing.

Chess pieces set up on a green park bench, the crowd leans in close watching him think, cardigan sweater with tortoise shell buttons, a cigarette juts out of thin lips, ash burning down, palsied hands and yellow nails …

Note that *plead* is an intransitive verb. It doesn't require a direct object, so *handkerchief* needs to stay in subject position. It could take an indirect object, introduced by a preposition: pleads *with*, pleads *for*… ."

Your turn.

Yup. Verbs. More tomorrow.

DAY #5

FINDING VERBS FROM NOUNS

Today I'll give you noun prompts, and you'll find a verb to create the collision. Again, don't just grab anything, but take your time and look for provocative, productive combinations. As you did yesterday, for each combination, write a sentence or short paragraph illuminating the metaphor. Then do a ninety-second piece of object writing, using the combination as the prompt.

Remember, the noun can also come after the verb as direct object, with another noun providing the subject.

Crossbow

JESS MEIDER

Crossbow *tongues*: The crossbow tongues arrows like a fire tongues a wick.

Soldiers scurry in ant chaotic style, red dots rampant, almost flamboyant across the dreary fields of Pennsylvania. Native crossbow; a quick and lethal ringing sound impales a young man's rib cage.

SUSAN CATTANEO

Crossbow *smiles*: A crossbow smiled with tension as the archer placed the arrow in place and pulled it back.

Horses stamp and whinny nervously, straw is crunchy underfoot, chain mail hangs heavy on the broad chest, vision narrowed in the metal helmet, the tickle of sweat trickling down back and neck, aiming out the parapet opening ...

The shape a crossbow takes when it's pulled back is like a smile. There's some real tension there, because the smile becomes sinister. When you tune your vision to metaphor, things like that jump out at you. And the arrow as a wick in the flame of a crossbow? Nice. Shapes are evocative. Notice them.

Your turn.

Kettle

BONNIE HAYES

Kettle *laughs*: The kettle laughs merrily on the stove and then shrieks its little song of readiness.

Outside, a chainsaw snorts and then cackles gleefully. A jay screams at some joke the squirrels tell him, and overhead, the clouds skip through the sky. My tea is hot and sweet, and day is clear, nothing hurts right now—for the moment, I'm happy.

SUSAN CATTANEO

Kettle *screeches*: The kettle screeches on the stove, a hot-aired harpy spewing steam.

Blue flames taunt her metal belly, the pillow of tea bag, a raspberry sachet, tossed into the steaming vat, water swirling with brown, hands cradle the china mug then pull away when the heat overwhelms ...

Once the kettle laughs, the entire Disney movie begins, with chainsaws, jays, and even clouds joining the orchestra. Next door at Susan's house, the kettle isn't quite as happy. Notice both Bonnie and Susan keyed into sound to find their verbs; keying into shape might have brought out something like *squats*.

Your turn.

Waitress __________

CHANELLE DAVIS

Waitress *battles*: The waitress battles to keep the heavy dinner plates on her arm as she weaves in and out of the overcrowded restaurant.

Waitress twists and turns, sucking in her stomach, squeezing through gaps, lifting plates almost above her head, hum of conversation, laughter, jazz band in the corner, clapping, pasta with creamy sauce and mussels ...

SUSAN CATTANEO

Waitress *storms*: The waitress storms the dining room, her hair a tornado of tinted blonde. She pours on the charm and flashes lightning white teeth.

Menus sticky with maple syrup, Elvis on the radio, eggs getting cold on the fry cook's metal counter, smell of bacon lingers in the air like mist, playing pick-up-sticks with toothpicks ...

Once Susan finds *storms*, other members of its family come rushing in to join the party. That's the beauty of collisions: each side brings entire families to elbow into the other's business.

Now, you try.

Summer __________

SUSAN CATTANEO

Summer *waltzes*: Summer waltzes on daisy feet across the open meadow's floor, sweeping away spring in the folds of her emerald gown.

A lone hawk circles and catches an updraft, bees lumber from flower to flower, a lizard bakes on a hot stone and then is gone, breathing in clover and overturned earth, a brook skips over …

ANN HALVERSON

Summer *buckles*: Summer buckles under the weight of wilting fruit, mounds of petals, lawns as far past thirsty as tumbleweeds.

Easter-blue sky and khaki horizon—but at night the light is yellow crime lamps, the air streaked with particles, shoes always white, breath clogging from a two minute run, the dust dried into in the seams of every joint, eating her …

I wonder what would happen if these were reversed: "_________ waltzes summer … ", "__________ buckles summer … ." Try it. Then do your own.

Graduation __________

CHANELLE DAVIS

Graduation *stretches*: Graduation stretches out across the afternoon, sighing during the final photos and lingering good-byes.

High heels sinking into the lawn, sipping champagne, face hurts from smiling for photos, itching to take off my black gown, holding pink roses …

SUSAN CATTANEO

Graduation *plods*: Four hundred graduates, three hours of speeches, ninety degrees in the shade… On hot, swollen and heavy feet, the graduation ceremony plods along through the dwindling afternoon.

Programs waving back and forth as makeshift fans, mosquitoes buzzing like miniature helicopters, hard wooden folding chairs, heels sinking into wet grass …

I didn't have the high-heel experience, though it must be a common experience, until now. Both Chanelle and Susan personify graduation, then give it an action. Nice.

Your turn.

More with verbs tomorrow. Exciting, yes?

DAY #6

FINDING NOUNS FROM VERBS

Yesterday was interesting, finding verbs from a noun prompt. Today you'll reverse that and find nouns from a verb prompt, nouns that create collisions with the verbs. This will be unfamiliar territory—it seems easier to know the noun and put it into action than to know the action and find something that does it. Or not, I'll let you judge.

As you did yesterday, for each combination, write a sentence or short paragraph about it. Then do your ninety-second piece of object writing.

VERBS

Flush

Indict

Paddle

Operate

Soar

______________ Flushes

CHANELLE DAVIS

***Company* flushes:** The company flushes out its underperforming staff in a recession.

Pulling the chain, swirling water, dirty waste, cold sterile porcelain bosses.

SUSAN CATTANEO

***Dusk* flushes:** Dusk flushes out the daylight, draining the color from the sunset and washing the sky clean.

Watercolor clouds drip on the horizon, streetlamps buzz on, the houses on the street huddle close in the silence, the moon is a hangnail in the dark …

What quality does *flush* have? It removes, gets rid of. So find some things that remove or are removed. Since *flush* is primarily a transitive verb—it asks for a direct object—you'll have to find two nouns: x flushes y. Dusk flushes daylight.

Hot spots: "porcelain bosses," "the moon is a hangnail in the dark."

Now, do your own.

______________ indicts

BONNIE HAYES

***Lilacs* indict:** The lilacs indict me with a few sparse flowers.

The garden is unhappy. My roses are reproachful, my iris refuse to bloom in their overcrowded beds. Even in my place of respite, I am coming up short.

SUSAN CATTANEO

***Gaze* indicts:** As he tiptoes in the back door at 5 a.m., her stern gaze indicts him, sentencing him to a long dawn of arguing.

Clock ticks by the stove, she paces the linoleum floor, nerves jangle like wind chimes, she hears his car in the distance, tires turning on gravel, he cuts the headlights, hoping their lighted eyes won't gaze in through the curtained windows.

Another transitive verb. Both Bonnie and Susan use a pronoun as a direct object. The collision is between the subject and the verb. The direct object comes along for the ride.

Your turn.

______________ Paddles

BONNIE HAYES

***Moon* paddles:** The moon paddles in a river of clouds streaming across the sky, bubbling up around it.

The stars are already underwater, drowning in the sudden flood of darkness, rising out of nowhere and obscuring the possibility of clarity on this night.

CHANELLE DAVIS

***Fire* paddles:** The fire paddles its way across the ground, waves of heat and embers are splashed amongst the native bush.

Moves quickly, helicopters buzzing with water buckets trying to stop the fire racing like a team of rowers, leaves a trail of smoky mist, coughing, burnt orange sky, flames drown the houses, flood the trees …

Aha! An intransitive verb. No direct object necessary, but you'll probably use a prepositional phrase like Bonnie and Chanelle did: "paddles *in* a river of clouds" and "fire paddles ... *across*."

Both use the water imagery that *paddles* suggests and apply it to the nouns' families with startling results.

Now, you try.

____________Operates

SUSAN CATTANEO

***Spider* operates:** The spider operates on its delicate web, threading the silk and stitching together nature's lace.

Monkeys chatter in trees, a mango yellow snake coils around a tree branch, footsteps crash in the undergrowth, a pioneer cuts boot prints in mud, rifle glinting in the blade of sun coming through the canopy of leaves.

ANN HALVERSON

***Rumor* operates:** Rumor operates as if it has its own army.

Its marching orders move the troops to every venue, battle ready, weapons sharpened for maximum result, responses set to engage and surprise and destroy. Sneaking into darkest spaces, leaving land mines of doubt behind them … the damage whispers in ears across barbed wire.

Hot spots: "rifle glinting in the blade of sun," "leaving land mines of doubt behind them."

Now, your turn.

______________ **soars**

BONNIE HAYES

***Party* soars:** The party soared around my ears, boosted by the wild energy of a full moon and kamikazes.

I could almost feel it in my hair, like wind, in the tingling of my fingertips like adrenaline. I let it lift me up and floated ever higher, with a kind of internal silence the way it might feel to be high high in the sky …

CHANELLE DAVIS

***Wasabi* soars:** The wasabi soars through my nose and into my brain, flapping around, trying to escape through the top of my scalp.

Scraping inside of my head, intense burning, pulsing shock waves, pecking my nose, scrunch up my face and hit my forehead with my fist trying to shake it out, watery eyes.

Soar, like *operate*, is intransitive. You understand the difference between transitive and intransitive verbs, right? Right.

Now, do your own.

You use lots of nouns and verbs in your writing. As in music, surprise at the right time matters. Find opportunities, when you have your noun, to audition a whole chorus line of verbs until you find an exciting collision. And conversely. It'll keep your writing fresh and interesting. You know how that is. You just did it for two days.

DAY #7

EXPRESSED IDENTITY: NOUN-NOUN COLLISIONS

Something new today. You'll work with expressed identity: noun colliding with noun. Remember the three forms of expressed identity:

1. x is y	A poem is a zipper
2. The y of x	The zipper of the poem
3. x's y	The poem's zipper

In your collisions today, try some of these constructions and see how they fit. Here are your nouns:

NOUNS	NOUNS
Wince	Cargo ship
Frisbee	Zipper
Poem	Evening
Summer	Captain
Restaurant	Wineglass

For each noun/noun combination, write a sentence or short paragraph. Then do your ninety seconds.

A wince is a cargo ship

SUSAN CATTANEO: She stubbed her bruised toe on the chair leg, and her wince was a cargo ship, holding a ten-ton pile of pain.

Ache radiating in waves, cutting through all other thoughts. Eyes dripping salty tears, she casts around her mind looking for a really good swearword to use ...

KRISTIN CIFELLI: Her wince was a cargo ship that hauled along emotions from years past. The sudden reaction, though quick and sharp, was also heavy with fear.

Trudging along through the dirty waters of your past, a slow reaction to fear, a wince, though quick and reactive, slows you down, full of heavy boxes of emotion, packed and stacked neatly inside your head ...

Note the water language in Susan's, drawn from the family of *cargo ship*. Kristin loads the ship with stacking boxes, cruising dirty waters. Note that Kristin's "the dirty waters of your past" is also an expressed identity is the second form, "the y of x," "your past is dirty waters."

Your turn.

A Frisbee is a zipper

GREG BECKER: The Frisbee flew through the air and zippered up the wind behind it as it spun itself forward.

Frisbee spinning wildly, crazy hippie disk toy on acid trip, barefoot flying from the patchouli fingers of torn jeans, grown child in the grassy sunny field of irresponsibility in the parking area for summer concert, with bandana dog chasing it, slobbering chewing it. Zipper on the hoodie of the Frisbee player with cracker and Dorito crumbs in the pockets …

KRISTIN CIFELLI: A Frisbee is a zipper that opens your grown-up world back to your kid planet.

With a simple toss of the Frisbee, he forgot all about the stress of his job, bills to be paid. The freeness of the Frisbee unzipped him from planet grown-up back to a fun and carefree kid-planet.

Both Greg and Kristin transformed *zipper* from a noun to a verb. Part of *zipper*'s family is the actions it can perform. Note Greg's "sunny field of irresponsibility," the second form of expressed identity, "irresponsibility is a sunny field." And Kristin's "planet grown-up," using an adjective-noun collision (*grown-up* is the adjective).

Now, try your own.

A poem is an evening

ANNE HALVORSEN: A poem is an evening on the front lawn.

First stanza myrtle green, quaggy underfoot with sinking toes in the new-mown smell renewed by a flash of thundershower; then four lines for the dusky, emerging dance of the two facing silhouettes … finally leaning in to lift and roll the frayed badminton net, taste of longing versed with after-rain, rhythms synched, first firefly fingers touch …

KRISTIN CIFELLI: A poem is an evening quietly settling your day inside you, and feeding you a hearty dinner.

Twilight—after the sun sets, the poem brings us to gorgeous gentle light, and eventually to starlight. Its rhymes and patterns are constellations of words in the night sky. Sparkling, twinkling …

Kristin's "Its rhymes and patterns are constellations of words in the night sky" creates two layers of expressed identity: The first version—*rhymes are constellations*—and the second version—*constellations of words*. A version of *words are constellations*. Anne's "taste of longing" is also a lovely example of the second version.

Your turn.

Summer is the captain

ANDREA STOLPE: Summer strode in as a decorated captain, marked by the stripes of all the knowledge and experience I'd accumulated during the year.

Come July I'd have T-shirt tan lines and wrinkles at the corners of my eyes from squinting in the blazing beach sun. This summer I'd avoid the french fry station and the burger flipping, and move right up into the position of lifeguard. I was sixteen, and all I wanted to feel was the sand dust layer on my toes and a stingy layer of salt. Grape slushes dripped down the chins of toddlers and …

SUSAN CATTANEO: Summer is the captain, ordering the daylight to stand at attention until way past 9 p.m.

Clouds march across the azure sky, mosquitoes hover on helicopter wings dive-bombing the man's white skin, traffic parades down main street …

Andrea becomes summer, and her ninety-second exercise gives an account of the stripes. Susan welcomes the military family into her ninety seconds. Nice.

You try.

A restaurant is a wineglass

ANNE HALVORSEN: A restaurant is a wineglass, its bouquet slipping out with satiated diners as she pulls open the door …

Standing at the top of spiral steps stemming from the round, darkened space, her eyes drinking in the open skylight, the streetlamps sparking the walls of glass … astonishing scents flooding her, loamy earth … a pastiche of sweet spice, baking bread, herbed oils, sliding her down the steps into the center of it all, eating the perfume even before she finds her feet enough to teeter toward her friends …

SUSAN CATTANEO: A restaurant is a wineglass, full of rosy patrons whose laughter spills over into the open streets …

Waiters flow through the crowded room, the chatter of silverware on china plates, music pours out from the speakers, the flicker of candlelight making crystal patterns on white tablecloths …

Both Anne and Susan invite the *wineglass* family into the restaurant. Find as many *wineglass* family members as you can in their pieces.

Now write your own.

DAY #8

EXPRESSED IDENTITY: NOUN-NOUN COLLISIONS

So now you're an old pro at expressed identity. Today, reverse the nouns and see what you can get.

NOUNS	NOUNS
Cargo ship	Wince
Zipper	Frisbee
Evening	Poem
Captain	Summer
Wineglass	Restaurant

As usual, write a sentence or short paragraph for each collision. Then do your ninety seconds.

A cargo ship is a wince

JESS MEIDER: The cargo ship's wince from the yellow explosion freeze its face into the night.

Seaside, I stand on tiny rocks, microscopic as they shift and shhh me while I shift my weight over bare feet. Sloshing in the distance, the lights of a bulldog-faced cargo ship wince, an explosive collision with another boat, baboom and billowing in the darkness, metal glugging in the seawater like an overthirsty beast.

BONNIE HAYES: A cargo ship is a wince on the otherwise placid and beautiful face of the ocean.

It shudders on the shoulders of the world and mars the peace, doing its quotidian tasks of making somebody money, while resting upon a world of miracles.

Note Jess's use of the third form of expressed identity, "cargo ship's wince." And Bonnie's introduction of face's family, including *shoulders*.

Your turn.

A zipper is a Frisbee

BONNIE HAYES: A zipper is a Frisbee, the traverser between up and down.

A yippee of energy. Up and down, over and over again, tracing its course, then suddenly off into the bushes or onto a busy street—ooops, caught; skin in the teeth!

CHANELLE DAVIS: Shoppers watched curiously as the tantrum escalated outside the supermarket. The mother and son played a game of Frisbee with his jacket zipper, which he refused to keep done up—stomping his feet in the blackened car park snow.

Metal zipping up and down, blue jacket cold numb fingers, red plastic boots, clanging of shopping trolleys, swishing of plastic grocery bags stretching under the weight of milk bottles, runny nose …

This one is trickier, but once you see that a Frisbee is in motion, back and forth, it's easier to see "the traverser between up and down" and the "game of Frisbee with his zipper." It's a game of looking for Frisbee qualities that are shared with zippers. Lots more on this later.

Write your own.

An evening is a poem

ANDREA STOLPE: An evening is a poem, strung along the infinite moment, harnessing dark and light, tangible and intangible.

Tufts of long grasses erupt from the fine sand at the edge of the trees, my spot for watching the earth descend into evening, and finally into deep sleep. Stars stud the night sky and I look across the Milky Way. The air thins as it cools, and my bare legs …

SUSAN CATTANEO: The winter evening is a poem, filled with chilly passages and the delicate cadence of snow flurries on the paper-white ground …

The wind breathing in and out in swirls of white powder, a dog crouches down then leaps into the snow, a four-legged iambic pentameter …

Hot spots: "poem *harnessing* dark and light"; "the delicate cadence of snow flurries."

Your turn.

The captain is summer

SUSAN CATTANEO: The army captain is summer, hot and sweaty in his fatigues, white and still while he waits for autumn to make the first move.

Languid trees lounge over his head, the jungle is a forest of green, combat boots squelch in the hazy mud …

KRISTIN CIFELLI: The captain is summer, with sandy blonde hair, Atlantic ocean-blue eyes, and glowing, carefree skin.

It was hard to take him seriously—the captain looked more like a lifeguard on Laguna Beach than an army captain. He was summer—carefree and all smiles, a friendly ice-cream cone, and a welcoming watermelon. He melted the girls with his sunny skin …

In this one a simile might make the direction clearer: "The captain is *like* summer, he … ."

It feels much easier to slide the other way—summer is a captain. That direction may offer more family members. When you have very few family members stepping into the other living room, simile may work better.

Both Susan and Kristin got it right, creating some pretty summery captains.

Now, you go.

A wineglass is a restaurant

SUSAN CATTANEO: Her wineglass was a restaurant, crowded with the taste of oak and pear, a transparent window to the wine sitting inside.

A mellow conversation in warm red, speaking of wide aisles of grapes, hanging full and ripe on the green curlicue vines, crushing pulp underfoot like sawdust, the bees are waiters hovering at each plant before moving on.

BONNIE HAYES: A wineglass is a restaurant full of smells and flavors.

Here is the smoke of the grill, the scent of the lilacs in the centerpieces, the berries in the compote. There is the bitterness of the greens, a slight smell of must from the area behind the bar, the mineral smell of money, and a slight tang of citrus.

This one works well both ways. Lots of family members in common—the mark of a productive metaphor. Clearly, both Susan and Bonnie know their wines.

Your turn.

DAY #9

EXPRESSED IDENTITY: FINDING NOUNS FROM NOUNS

Okay, today you'll start with a noun and find an expressed identity of your own.

Start by surveying some members of the prompt's family and see what other families they might belong to. You'll become very familiar with this process in Challenge #3. This is the ramp to get you there safely.

Find a colliding noun for each of the nouns below and write your sentence or short paragraph. Then do your ninety seconds.

Maple tree is ________

CAROLINE HARVEY: The maple tree is an *elephant.*

It is hefty and anchored into the ground, swinging its branches in the spring breeze, swaying its bark trunk and sauntering heavily; bristly to the touch, rough hewn and covered in dirt. Slow, steady, and it remembers you as a child, climbing it with your sweaty palms and smooth feet.

GREG BECKER: The maple tree is *the grandfather of the backyard.*

Maple tree strong and old unwilling to budge, releasing its sap through the spikes that have been stuck in it, the old bull in the ring with swords dangling from its back and blood trickling down them as the sweet nectar of the maple tree is stolen by our greedy sweet tooth—the wise old maple tree weathered years of storms and fierce winds.

The *elephant* family has lots of members to choose from. I especially like "it remembers you as a child, climbing it with your sweaty palms and smooth feet," and "the wise old maple tree weathered years of storms."

Write your own.

Traffic is ________

CHARLOTTE PENCE: The traffic is *desire stutter-stopping down Broadway.*

A scarf, a hair band, a tinny umbrella spoke ground down into the asphalt where you wait in this stalled dance of desire that groans and honks and birds and slices to the right. Each car is a link, an animal with its own whirring engine and downshift grit. The wheel under your hands is too smooth and the sky above you narrows to the width of your lane. And in your mouth is the taste of dry chrome as you inch up only to stop again, moving in an idling path of smoke, horns.

CAROLINE HARVEY: The *hawk* of traffic flies by my LA apartment at vibrating speeds.

My couch rattles and I can hear the whoosh of cars, the honk of impatient horns, smell the toxic grey of smog. Somewhere there is an ocean; salty crystal waiting to dry on my skin and in my hair; somewhere there is sunshine waiting to color my skin with warmth. But here, in this apartment, there is only the zip of traffic's wings, rushing past me on its way to kill, cars moving in an orchestrated hunt.

Hot spots: "this stalled dance of desire that groans and honks" and "the zip of traffic's wings, rushing past me on its way to kill." Note Charlotte's use of the second version of expressed identity, "dance of desire," and Caroline's "the hawk of traffic."

Your turn.

Sunrise is ________

CHANELLE DAVIS: Sunrise is a *volcano.*

A volcano of sunrise erupted across the horizon.

Orange and yellow light, lava flowing into the sky, taking over the land, slowly warming my skin, drying out dew on grass, rooster crowing …

GREG BECKER: Sunrise is a *symphony.*

The twill of the tiny robin was the first note of the sunrise symphony.

The slow steady climb of the sun, as it approaches the night sky over the horizon the world begins tuning up and preparing for its arrival at the horizon the symphony begins growing with birds, dogs, car doors …

Chanelle asked the color members of *sunrise*'s family to help find another noun: What else splashed orange, gold, and yellow into the sky? Ah yes, a *volcano.* Greg focused on *sunrises*'s sounds and arrived at *symphony.* Not so hard ...

Now, you try.

Cathedral is ________

SUSAN CATTANEO: The cathedral's *eyes* sparkled in the evening sun as its stained glass pupils took in the city below.

White stone skin and head of spires, looming tall and statuesque over the smaller red roofs, God's beauty queen looking down on her subjects ...

CHANELLE DAVIS: The cathedral is a *kaleidoscope* of colour and beauty.

Sun shining through stained glass ceiling, rainbows of colour, I look up and spin around on the marble floor, patterns blurring and repeating, changing with the light ...

Susan took an extra step: The cathedral is a person, a person has eyes thus the cathedral's eyes—the third form of expressed identity. Chanelle focuses on the multicolored cathedral and made it to something else multicolored. She could easily have used the third version of expressed identity, the *cathedral's kaleidoscope*.

Your turn.

Policeman is ________

CHANELLE DAVIS: The policeman is an *owl*, the way he swoops through the dark streets on his motorbike, wide-eyed and alert, hunting down the runaway prisoner ...

Moves quick, swerving, taking tight corners, leaning on his bike, stopping to peer over fences and scan trees, dark camouflaged jacket and pants, silent and ...

KRISTIN CIFELLI: The policeman is *electricity for the city*, keeping it lit up, making it run, and speeding through the streets to save the day.

Policeman—strong, there for you quickly, rescuing you from darkness. sparking goodness and electrocuting danger. Flying through the streets with a charge ...

Chanelle sees the policeman hunting. What else hunts? Kristin sees the policeman keeping the city running. What else makes the city run? Easy, eh?

Your turn.

DAY #10

PLAYING IN KEYS: USING LINKING QUALITIES

Today, you'll go beyond what you've just done and explore the process of finding metaphors in deeper detail. You'll be working with three prompts and will be asked to create two responses for each one—six explorations in all. Take your time.

First, the following lesson, from the second edition of my book, *Writing Better Lyrics*. It takes a closer look at the concept that words belong to *families* or *keys*.

PLAYING IN KEYS

Like musical notes that belong to the same key, words can group together in family relationships. Call this a "diatonic relationship." For example, here are some random words that are diatonic to (in the same key as) *tide:* ocean, moon, recede, power, beach.

This is "playing in the key of tide," where tide is the fundamental tone. This is a way of creating collisions between elements that have at least some things in common—a fertile ground for metaphor. There are many other keys *tide* can belong to when something else is a fundamental tone, for example, *power.* Let's play in its key: Muhammad Ali; avalanche; army; Wheaties; socket; tide.

All of these words are related to each other by virtue of their relationship to "power." If you combine them into little collisions, you can often discover metaphors:

> Muhammad Ali avalanched over his opponents.
> An avalanche is an army of snow.
> This army is the Wheaties of our revolution.
> Wheaties plug your morning into a socket.
> A socket holds back tides of electricity.

Try playing in the key of *moon*: stars, harvest, lovers, crescent, astronauts, calendar, tide.

> The New Mexico sky is a rich harvest of stars.
>
> Evening brings a harvest of lovers to the beach.
>
> The lovers' feelings waned to a mere crescent.
>
> The crescent of human knowledge grows with each astronaut's mission.
>
> Astronauts' flights are a calendar of human courage.
>
> A new calendar washes in a tide of opportunities.

Essentially, metaphor works by revealing some third thing that two ideas share in common. One good way of finding metaphors is by asking these two questions:

1. What characteristics does my idea (*tide*) have?
2. What else has those characteristics?

Answering the second question usually releases a flood of possible metaphors.

Often the relationship between two ideas is not clear. *Muhammad Ali* is hardly the first idea that comes to mind with *avalanche*, unless you recognize their linking term, *power*. In most contexts, *Muhammad Ali* and *avalanche* are nondiatonic, or unrelated to each other. Only when you look for a link do you come up with *power*, or *deadly*, or "*try to keep quiet when you're in their territories*." Asking the two questions:

1. What quality does my object have?
2. What else has that quality?

Okay, start by listing policeman qualities. Here's one:

He protects.

What else protects?

Now find two other things that *protect*. Then find related nouns, verbs, and adjectives for each member of the list and try to apply them to *policeman*. Write a sentence or a short paragraph for the good ones.

CHANELLE DAVIS

1. Flu Vaccine

2. Lifeguard

Flu Vaccine: needle, injections, nurse, doctor, veins, immunize, blood, cure, medicine, prick, hospital, cough, sickness, mucus, winter

The police immunize the public and help fight the symptoms of gangs in New York.

Lifeguard: drowning, waves, rip, sea, beach, swimming, uniform, swift, strong, muscly, watchful, on duty

The police were watchful after the earthquake and rescued many stores from the waves of looters that flooded the city.

Your turn. List two of your own things that *protect*. Then find related nouns, verbs, and adjectives for each one and try to apply them to *policeman*. Write a sentence or a short paragraph for the ones you like.

What else does a policeman do?

He *investigates*.

What else investigates?

KRISTIN CIFELLI: *X-ray*

X-ray: black and white, broken bones, revealing, diagnose

The police are an x-ray, investigating the broken bones of the neighborhood, revealing every fracture in black and white.

What else investigates?

CHARLIE WORSHAM: *mechanic*

Mechanic: engine, oil, sweat, heat, grease, dirty, smudged, pistons, wrench, fans, belts, whirring, motor, crank, hood

Policemen are the mechanics of mystery. They roll up their sleeves, wipe their brow, and pop open the hood of a criminal case, hoping to unlock the mystery. Every

piston that misfires, every loose fan belt, every drop of oil is a fingerprint, a smoking gun, a clue as to what went wrong and who's to blame. In the workshop of a downtown office building or crime lab, they take apart and rebuild every piece of the machine. Whatever it takes, they don't stop till they can prosecute the bad guy. And like years of sweat equity beneath the workings of vehicles, years of experience with all makes and models of crimes, train a professional policeman to spot likely suspects quickly and efficiently.

Your turn. List two other things that *investigate*, then find related nouns, verbs, and adjectives for each member of the list. Try to apply them to *policeman*. Write a sentence or a short paragraph for the good ones.

What else does a policeman do?

He arrests.

What else arrests?

CHANELLE DAVIS: *Heart*

Heart: stop beating, death, hospital, electric shock, blood, circulation, ambulance, dying

More police were pumped into the undercover operation, aiming to stop the circulation of pornography.

CAROLINE HARVEY: *The loudest sound you can imagine*

The loudest sound you can imagine: makes everything else disappear, stops time, terrifies, echoes, makes your ears numb and ringing, makes everything after feel silent and small, makes you flinch

When I saw him stand up, the rest of the courtroom disappeared. I couldn't feel my legs, my hands were dangling at my side like a shaky mess of Parkinson's. He thundered to the witness chair, his feet thumping loudly with every gait. I cannot remember anything else from that day, but I can recall exactly the way he adjusted first his left shirt sleeve and then his right. How his hair was parted just a few degrees of center and shone under the fluorescent lights like Superman's pompadour. The sound of his voice, as he answered my attorney's questions, echoed the way I imagine a blow hom might sound in the Grand Canyon. All living creatures living miles within distance of the courthouse were silenced when he spoke. When he finished and was excused, I looked down at my hands. I was gripping the fabric of my flowered dress and my left knee, jittery as a mosquito, was helpless.

Your turn. List two other things that *arrest*, then find related nouns, verbs, and adjectives for each member of the list. Try to apply them to *policeman*. Write a sentence or a short paragraph for the good ones.

DAY #11

PLAYING IN KEYS: USING LINKING QUALITIES

Okay, here you go again. Today you'll be working with two prompts and will be asked to create two responses for each one—four explorations in all. Take your time.

Start with the noun *cathedral*. Here are some qualities:

It inspires.

What else inspires?

SUSAN CATTANEO: *Moon*

Moon inspires: astronaut, mysterious, faraway, remote, glowing, controlling tides, waxing, waning, eclipse

The cathedral eclipsed the other buildings in the city and its congregation waxes and wanes depending on people's need for faith.

Music inspires: flowing, in time, rhythmic, scored, fluid, toe tapping, expressive, cadenced

The cathedral rose up from the street, a melody in fluid stone that harmonized beautifully with its stained glass windows.

CHANELLE DAVIS: *Teacher*

Teacher inspires: knowledge, learning, patient, wise, keeper, books, information, instructs, delivers, pass on, link, education, school, old

The cathedral is a patient teacher, linking generations with divine knowledge.

Your turn. List two other things that *inspire*, then find related nouns, verbs, and adjectives for each member of the list. Try to apply them to *cathedral*. Write a sentence or a short paragraph for the good ones.

Here's another quality of a cathedral:

Being at the pinnacle.

What else is *at the pinnacle?*

SUSAN CATTANEO: *The Super Bowl*

St. Peter's Cathedral is the Super Bowl of churches, dominating over the city, a giant spectacle for all to see.

KRISTIN CIFELLI: *Rolls-Royce*

Decorated in Michelangelo frescoes, and bigger-than-life-sized marble statues, St. Peter's Cathedral is a Rolls Royce: expensive, bursting with pride and status, and only to be used for extremely special occasions.

Now, your turn. Write your own.

DAY #12

PLAYING IN KEYS: FINDING LINKING QUALITIES

Once again, you'll respond to two prompts. List at least three qualities for each prompt. Then, for each quality in your list, ask, "What else has that quality?" and look for related nouns, verbs, and adjectives, and apply them as usual. Write a sentence or a short paragraph for each one.

Maple Tree

ANDREA STOLPE: *Is beloved*

What else has that quality?

A family heirloom: worn as jewelry, precious, vintage

The maple tree is a family heirloom, draping around the neck of the lush green yard.

CHANELLE DAVIS: *Changes colour*

What else has that quality?

Woman: makeup, blusher, eye shadow, dress up, naked, beauty, elegance

The maple tree slowly undressed herself to reveal pale smooth skin, her red dress gathered around her feet.

SUSAN CATTANEO: *It sprouts*

What else has that quality?

Rumors: tongues wagging, painful words, whispered behind backs, the cut of the words, tattletale, gossip, secrets

The maple tree gossiped with the wind, leaves whispering secrets about the coming autumn.

Go ahead and list three qualities of a maple tree.

Now ask, "What else has that quality?" and look for nouns, verbs, and adjectives related to the new object, and apply them as usual. Write a sentence or a short paragraph for each one

Here's your second noun to work with:

Traffic

What quality does traffic have?

ANDREA STOLPE: *It's congested*

What else has that quality?

Congested: Nose, bulbous, pointed, used for smelling

The traffic was an allergenic nose, a bulbous stack of congestion along the wrinkled highway.

SUSAN CATTANEO: *It's slow*

What else has that quality?

Old man: baggy pressed pants, wisps of gray hair, yellowed teeth, wheezing, shuffling feet, stooped shoulders, a folded newspaper under his arm, sensible shoes

Wheezing exhaust, the traffic shuffled along, its stooped shoulders resigned to waiting.

KRISTIN CIFELLI: *Honking*

Trumpet: blare, toot, symphony, ducks on a pond

The traffic plays a symphony of horns, honking, in three movements that seem never-ending.

Go ahead and list three qualities of traffic.

Asking, "What else has that quality?" look for nouns, verbs, and adjectives related to your qualities, and apply them as usual. Write a sentence or a short paragraph for each one.

DAY #13

PLAYING IN KEYS: FINDING LINKING QUALITIES

Again today you'll respond to two prompts. List at least three qualities for each prompt, and for each quality in your list, ask, "What else has that quality?" and look for related nouns, verbs, and adjectives and apply them as usual. Write a sentence or a short paragraph for each one.

Here's the first one:

Handshake

CHANELLE DAVIS:

strong
gestures peace
congratulates

What else has that quality?

Sumo wrestlers: Fat, sweat, heavy wrestling, locked in, gripping

The businessmen shook hands, sumo wrestlers gripping each other tightly, each trying to tip the other off his feet.

White flag: wind, peace, flapping, cloth

The handshake is a white flag, flapping briefly in the winds of peace.

Gold medal: shine, first place, winning, sports event, race

The handshake was a gold medal at the end of a long race to win the development contract.

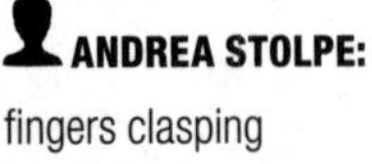

ANDREA STOLPE:

fingers clasping
confident
final

What else has that quality?

Lovers: honeymoon, naive, poetry

A handshake is lover's poetry, fingers clasping in a honeymoon of beautiful imagery.

A lawyer: argumentative, bends truths, secretive

A handshake argues with the confidence of a lawyer, overruling anyone who might challenge its final word.

A parent's word: strict, non-negotiable, must be obeyed

A handshake parents an arrangement with a strict and unwavering decree.

Now, go ahead and list three qualities of a handshake.

Asking, "What else has that quality?" look for nouns, verbs, and adjectives related to your qualities and apply them as usual. Write a sentence or a short paragraph for each one.

Okay, here's your second noun:

Sunrise

CHANELLE DAVIS: *It's slow*

What else has that quality?

Rosebud: petals, unfolding, bloom, scent, bees, pollen, stem, leaves, garden

The sunrise began as a tiny bud, slowly unfolding its petals of red light into the morning sky.

CHARLIE WORSHAM: *It ignites*

What else has that quality?

Match: explode, burn, set fire, flame, scratch, sulfur, cardboard box, cigarette, flicker

A sunrise is the strike of a match: that first burst of light exploding in the atmosphere, setting fire to the day.

SUSAN CATTANEO: *It's beautiful*

What else has that quality?

Princess: golden hair, silk gown, dainty slippers, eyes flashing, full red lips

The sunrise lifted her dainty skirt and tiptoed over the mountain, placing one satin toe of light into the darkened valley.

Your turn. Go ahead and list three qualities of a sunrise,

Asking, "What else has that quality?" look for nouns, verbs, and adjectives related to your qualities, and apply them as usual. Write a sentence or a short paragraph for each one.

There's nothing mysterious about finding metaphor. It's a step-by-step search that yields positive results in most cases. Expressed identity is a great diving board, plunging you into a pool of possibilities. Simply keep your eyes open under water. There are lots of things to see.

DAY #14

SIMILE

Before moving on to the next challenge, you'll take a look at simile.

You learned in high school that the difference between metaphor and simile is that simile uses *like* or *as*. Of course, it also uses *than*. True enough, but that's like saying that measles are spots on your body. They are, but if you look deeper, the spots are there because a virus is present. There is something more fundamental going on.

Samuel Taylor Coleridge called metaphor "an act of the imagination," whereas he relegated simile to "an act of fancy." He identified the difference between metaphor and simile as a difference of degree, depending on how much the two ideas shared in common. If they shared only a few, simile. More, metaphor.

This would be a candidate for simile:

> Like a lobster boil'd, the morn
> From black to red began to turn
>
> —SAMUEL BUTLER

A boiled lobster doesn't have much in common with morning except that they both change from black to red: The morning sunrise reddens the sky, the boiled lobster turns from black to red as it cooks. Metaphor wouldn't work here:

> Morning is a boiled lobster
> The boiled lobster of the morning
> Morning's boiled lobster

While in metaphor, the two terms share several qualities. It's perhaps a good guideline for choosing between metaphor and simile, but I prefer making the choice in terms of commitment.

Love is a rose.

Where do you focus? On the second term?

Love = **rose**

Or the first term?

Love = rose

If you want the texture, smell, color of the rose in focus, use metaphor.

Love is a **rose**.

If you want love as the focus, use simile:

Love is like a rose.

Simile doesn't transfer focus: *like* works as an energy blocker—it reflects energy back onto the first term, refusing to let the energy pass to the second term. The *is* of metaphor allows free passage of energy to the second term, and lights it up.

Freedom is riding a bike for the first time without help.

The energy is transferred to the bike rider here. You see her wobbling down the sidewalk, a breathless parent smiling and gasping as he watches her pull further away—a harbinger of things to come.

Freedom is like riding a bike for the first time without help.

Here you stay focused on the concept of freedom. Maybe you reflect a bit on the feeling you had when you first rode your bike alone, but muttering the conclusion, "Yup, that's what freedom is like."

Simile is an excellent tool for working with abstract concepts like freedom or emotions like hope, trust, or bitterness. A way of making them specific. Of course, metaphor is a perfect vehicle for those purposes, too.

Like has a bad reputation these days. Its legitimate uses are either as a verb

I like the smell of evening.

Or to introduce simile.

Like the smell of evening …

Unfortunately, our culture has co-opted it to be used as an interruptor, causing me to write the following lyric:

LEAVE MY LIKE ALONE

Pat Pattison/Greg Barnhill

Like clouds that lace the open sky high above Nevada
Like dust behind the horses on the dry plains of Montana
Like thunder in the summer in the hills outside Atlanta
The pictures that I like come rolling by

But like, I don't like like when it's like used like it's like nothing
Like I don't like like when it's like used instead of said
Like, "she's like, no way," "he's like OK"
Man like that's so like not my tone
Now won't you just LEAVE MY LIKE ALONE
Yeah LEAVE MY LIKE ALONE

I like the smell at evening when the dew is on the grasses
I like the songs of ice cream trucks weaving past like laughter
And little children clutching quarters, like the memories they gather
I like to go there every time I close my eyes

So like, I don't like like when it's like used like it's like nothing
Like I don't like like when it's like used instead of said
Like, "she's like, no way," "he's like OK"
Man like that's so like not my tone

Now won't you just LEAVE MY LIKE ALONE

Like somewhere in the valley girls abandon their vocabularies
Total conversations made of only so and like
And it's so hard to distinguish
When you murder the king's English
So like I wrote this little song, I thought I'd try because

You see, I don't like like when it's like used like it's like nothing
Like I don't like like when it's like used instead of said
Like, "she's like, no way," "he's like OK"
Man like that's so like not my tone
Now won't you just LEAVE MY LIKE ALONE
Please just LEAVE MY LIKE ALONE

**Find the complete song at patpattison.com under "patsongs."*

Today you'll be working with simile. You'll be asked to find three similes for each term, plus a description explaining the connections. Like this:

Thirst is like a guest who won't go away.

You can bear it for a while, but the longer you wait, the more uncomfortable you feel, until you finally have to head for the bathroom and close the door.

Thirst is like a buffalo hunter on the dry plains of Montana.

It stalks everywhere, looking for prey to bring down, peering through tumbleweed at figures moving in the distance toward the waterhole. If it has its way it'll stop them cold before they can get there.

Being thirsty is like being the parent of a teenage daughter.

Always wanting another little drop of information and attention, in the dry landscape of texting and sleepovers, after the waterfall of affection from childhood has long since turned to a trickle.

Your turn. Find three similes for each of the following terms. Then write a short elaboration on each one.

Trust is like:

1. Trust is like a good night's sleep. It allows your mind to rest, and you can rely on it. **—CHARLIE WORSHAM**

2. Trust is like a patchwork quilt, made from swatches and squares of people and experiences. It is many colors, many patterns, and frayed at the edges. Over the years it lies threadbare, but still provides warmth and comfort in the cold of life. **—ANDREA STOLPE**

3. Trust is like a roof. You don't really notice it until it's gone. **—MO McMORROW**

Now you try. What is trust like?

A bad joke is like:

1. A bad joke is like a penny you drop that falls through an open grate on the sidewalk. For the joke teller, it is more an embarrassment than a true loss. **—CHARLIE WORSHAM**

2. A bad joke is like a fart in an elevator. You are forced to politely stand there and sniff it in until the door opens. **—CHANELLE DAVIS**

3. A bad joke is like spilled milk, spreading over the tablecloth of conversation, drowning the napkins. You try mopping up the white and milky liquid, but it has already started to seep into the wood of the table, smelling more and more sour. **—SUSAN CATTANEO**

Now you try. What is a bad joke like?

Divorce is like:

1. Divorce is like a fighter pilot's ejector seat. When the marriage is going down in flames, press the button for a second chance.**—CHANELLE DAVIS**

2. Divorce is like a bushfire. Without it some trees don't seed. **—MO McMORROW**

3. Divorce is like a car crash: Anger like twisted metal, the ambulance comes too late to save anyone, the pavement is strewn with old memories, the same arguments like the same turn in the road that you always take too fast. **—SUSAN CATTANEO**

Your turn. What is divorce like?

A waterfall is like:

1. A waterfall is like a bridal veil, white and flowing down the smooth back of the rocks. **—CHANELLE DAVIS**

2. A waterfall is like hair, falling in luscious strands off the rocky head of the cliff, made gold in the sunlight, smooth until it hits the bottom in a froth of curls, the whitewater rafts have oars that comb through the currents. **—SUSAN CATTANEO**

3. A waterfall is like a construction worker. Pounding and jackhammering the stone face of the mountain, gallons of raw strength pour over the cliff. **—ANDREA STOLPE**

Your turn. What is a waterfall like?

Hope is like:

1. Hope is like a teddy bear, comforting to hold onto, squeezing it tightly when you're afraid, and helping you rest your head to sleep at night. **—KRISTIN CIFELLI**

2. Hope is like spandex, stretching across the flab of life. The wider the challenge, the thinner it becomes, but it will take more than a pint of melted dreams to split the seams of this stargazer. **—ANDREA STOLPE**

3. Hope is like a faithful dog. It guards your dreams and walks two paces in front until you get to your destination. **—CHANELLE DAVIS**

Your turn. What is hope like?

Wow! Congratulations! You've finished the metaphor challenge and should be seeing the world with new vision, or at least, I hope so. You are well-prepared for the third challenge, which entails going deeper into metaphor and learning to extend and manipulate it.

Take a little time off, if you'd like. You've earned it. Let these ways of looking seep into your bloodstream. Don't be gone too long, though. The next challenge is fun and will keep you moving forward. You will cross boundaries you may not have seen before.

CHALLENGE #3

OBJECT WRITING WITH METAPHOR

★ ★ ★ ★ ★ ★ ★ ★ ★ ★ ★ ★ ★ ★ ★

I would hurl words into this darkness and wait for an echo, and if an echo sounded, no matter how faintly, I would send other words to tell, to march, to fight, to create a sense of hunger for life that gnaws in us all.

—RICHARD WRIGHT, *AMERICAN HUNGER*

This challenge is an extension and continuation of the metaphor challenge. You've accomplished quite a bit so far, writing from your senses and learning to use your images—the stuff of your senses—to be seen as something more: William Faulkner's crowded cans of sardines on the country store shelf become the crowd of people in the general store watching the trial of Abner Snopes, accused of burning a barn.

Now for the next step.

What quality does a can of sardines have? Crowded. What else is crowded? The shelf, crowded with crowded things. The courtroom, crowded with the townsfolk.

The courtroom = can of sardines

In what respect?

They're both crowded.

So now I get to use nouns, verbs, and adjectives that really belong with, say, *can of sardines* and apply them to *the courtroom*.

The courtroom felt packed in oil
The courtroom felt dead and gray
The courtroom, layered in townsfolk
The oily courtroom
Something fishy ...

Faulkner chose to put cans of sardines on the shelf for a reason: It was ultimately a metaphor for Abner's quest to break free of any kind of restriction. Pretty cool.

Essentially, to find a metaphor you find some quality that two separate ideas share in common. The best way is to ask these two questions:

1. What interesting quality does my idea have?
2. What else has that quality?

Answering the second question usually releases a flood of possible metaphors.

In this fourteen-day challenge you're going to exercise your ability to extend metaphors—to find more and more common links between the two ideas of the metaphor (the courtroom = can of sardines), and to be able to transpose the qualities of one onto the other: to talk about the courtroom in fishy, oily, packed language.

You'll be asked to respond each day with object writing that stays deep in the senses, but the object writing in this section, unlike the writing you've done up to this point, can be focused on a more unified narrative thread.

For the first seven days, I'll supply the **linking qualities**—the qualities that will serve as links to a new idea, which I'll call the **target idea**. Starting on day eight, you'll be asked to find your own linking qualities, from which you'll find your **target idea** (what else has that quality?). You'll be asked each day to do ten-minute pieces of object writing for each pairing.

Fear not. As usual, each day will include two example responses from other writers, including poets, songwriters, and prose writers. Go get 'em.

★ ★ ★ ★ ★

DAY #1

LINKING QUALITIES TO TARGET IDEAS

Prompt: Snowstorm

You see a *snowstorm* and wonder what it could be a metaphor for. Usually, you see something about it—a *quality*—that reminds you of something else, like how the flakes float to the ground. Your mind makes the leap to other things that float to the ground, and you might think of autumn leaves. You start to think of how snowstorms are like falling leaves, or how falling leaves are like snowstorms. Wow, you think, a blizzard of leaves, or, the sky shedding snow. You can think of either one in terms of the other. And what made it possible was linking from snowstorm, through its quality, *floating to the ground,* to leaves. That's usually how it happens.

But, rather than waiting for inspiration and for those "aha" moments to occur, you can make a habit of seeing one thing through the lens of something else; it can become a way of looking at the world. That's what writers do—see the world on several levels. They're always combing snowstorms and crashing waves for metaphors.

You start by asking: What interesting qualities does *snowstorm* have? Here are a few:

Cold
Covering the ground

Hot cider by the fireplace
Slippery roads
Low visibility

I'll call these qualities of *snowstorm* the **linking qualities**. They'll provide the link from *snowstorm* to a new idea, which I'll call the **target idea**—the idea that *snowstorm* can be a metaphor *for.*

Start with *cold.*

A snowstorm is cold. You can now look for what *snowstorm* can be a metaphor for by asking: What else is *cold?*

You're searching for your **target idea**.

How about *your sneer?* It's pretty cold.

Snowstorm → Linking quality: *Cold* → Target idea: *Your sneer*

And now, after linking the quality *cold* to the target idea, *your sneer,* you'll take ten minutes to explore *your sneer* through the lens of *snowstorm,* describing the sneer in snowy qualities. Like this:

Your sneer is a snowstorm.

I stiffen up, muscles tensing as I watch your face contort into a cold sneer. Frigid blast, pushing me back on my heels, your words pelting me, my eyes tearing against the chill. I feel your contempt piling up around me, a shiver running down my back in goose bumps, while you lean in, immobilizing me in your icy landscape; I'm frozen, unable to move my legs. My heart, racing, begins to slow, blood thickening, dimming into silence.

So I've moved from *snowstorm* to *cold* to *your sneer,* which led to a description of our fight and its effect on me. You weren't very nice ...

Now try the second linking quality, *covering the ground:*

Snowstorm → Linking quality: *Covering the ground* → Target idea: *Wildflowers*

And now, after linking the quality *covering the ground* to the target idea, *wildflowers,* you'll take ten minutes to explore *wildflowers* through the lens of *snowstorm,* describing the wildflowers in snowy qualities. Like this:

A storm of wildflowers

> A meadow of reds, purples, golds, and yellows, blanketing the earth, a storm of perfumed color, making you blink and breathe deep. Pollen swirling, like snowflakes dancing in the air, melting into petals that will soon float onto the thick grass, nourishing the hungry soil. A riot of chirping and crickets, snow white clouds sailing overhead …

So I've moved from *snowstorm* to *covering the ground* to *wildflowers*, leading to a description of a meadow covered by flowers. Pretty. A positive look at the snowstorm for a change.

How about *hot cider by the fireplace?*

> **Snowstorm** → Linking quality: *Hot cider by the fireplace* → Target idea: *Seeking comfort*

A snowstorm seeking comfort

Take ten minutes to explore *seeking comfort* through the lens of *snowstorm*. Like this:

> Surge forward in your dress of white, loose and flowing, moan and push on, muscles coiled, straining. Breathe deep, great gulps opening your throat, feeling the howl rise from your toes, screaming up through your chest and through your cracked lips. Taste the doors clamped tight against you, fearing you—cold, bitter. Push hard in your dress of white until your pulse hammers and you sag, melting finally to the ground.

So I've moved from *snowstorm* to *hot cider by the fireplace* to *seeking comfort*, which led to the description, perhaps, of a pretty scary woman rampaging through a town. Or not. You could be talking right to the storm as though it were a woman crying out for comfort. Either way works great! Fun, eh?

Try this out. Following the examples above, supply the target idea for each of the linking qualities below:

> Snowstorm → Linking quality: *Slippery roads* → Target idea: _____________

What else has slippery roads? A high school? A relationship? Take ten minutes to explore your own target idea through the lens of *snowstorm*. Remember to stay as locked into sense-bound language as you can. First, here are a couple of examples.

ROB GILES

Snowstorm → Linking quality: *Slippery roads* → Target idea: *Argument*

An argument is a snowstorm.

Your cold shoulder and my heated anger smashed together in midair over the kitchen table. Like ice cracking beneath our feet, we heard too late to escape what was coming. We'd rather die than escape it seemed, so we stomped our feet against our fate, desperate to be heard, as each pressing point piled up, silently, but in a wall of cold hard snow around our hearts. We could not see each other in the flurry of our insistence. We would never find our way back to where we came from—back into the warmth of our hearth, the comfort of our home where we used to see eye to eye, hear each other's perspectives, love each other even when we disagreed. And the pressure built, thicker clouds rolled in, and before we knew it we were self-abandoned in the darkening woods, losing feeling in our fingers and toes, our cheeks and noses; we had too little on and were too far from safety, and worse of all we were not helping each other to stay safe. No bread crumbs were to be found under these drifts, no echo to give us bearings, our screams were swallowed up by the slow white blanket that dangerously drifted in to bury us. Together or apart, we were lost, both helplessly holding pieces of a map that lead in different directions. The sun setting on us and the temperature dropping, we were doomed by our pride as our argument buried us alive.

Rob holds open house for *snowstorm*'s family members, seeing his target idea, *argument* through the lens of *snowstorm*. In doing so, he extends the metaphor, digging deep into *snowstorm*'s family tree. Take a little time and underline as many as you can.

MICHAEL SHORR

Snowstorm → Linking quality: *Slippery roads* → Target idea: *Marriage*

Marriage is a snowstorm.

I can see the blizzard coming. The clouds of growing anger begin to darken your lovely face. My stomach fills with icy dread. You speak and in your trying-to-stay-calm voice I hear the building storm, a distant howling, frozen flakes of love begin to fall in the air between us. The wide-open, clear blue sky of our happiness grows pale, then gray, then the storm unleashes and explodes, warm love disintegrates into stabbing horizontal sheets of stinging curses and hurled accusations, like a frozen sandstorm, pelting my skin, freezing my tenderness. I wince and bend and curl my body into a ball—backing away—like I'm huddling into a thick, warm coat trying to protect myself from the frozen assault, the machine gun of icy attack.

Michael uses the second version of expressed identity here with "clear blue sky of our happiness grows pale." Note also his use of verbal metaphor and adjective/noun in "warm love disintegrates" and his final simile, "curl my body into a ball—backing away—like I'm huddling into a thick, warm coat trying to protect myself."

Your turn. What else has slippery roads? Take ten minutes to explore your target idea through the lens of *snowstorm*. Again, remember to stay as locked into sense-bound language as you can.

Snowstorm → Linking quality: *Slippery roads* → Target idea:______________

Okay, here's your next linking quality to work with:

Snowstorm → Linking quality: *Low visibility* → Target idea: ______________

What else has low visibility? Take ten minutes to explore your target idea through the lens of *snowstorm*. Again, remember to stay as locked into sense-bound language as you can.

TAMI NEILSEN

Snowstorm → Linking quality: *Low visibility* → Target idea: *Prejudice*

Prejudice is a snowstorm.

You've already made up your mind about who I am and nothing I say or do can make you see me. Your flurry of cold opinions swirl furiously, blinding your eyes and snowing me under with white, oppressive silence. There's an episode of *Little House on the Prairie*, the one with the big snowstorm, where Pa Ingalls ties a rope to the barn to try and feel his way back home, but the blizzard is so dense, he can't find his bearings—those things he knows are true and real. I always wondered how he could have gotten so terribly lost in such a short distance. With teeth chattering, chilled to the bone by your ignorance, now I know.

A wonderful, fresh look at the abstract concept, *prejudice*. This process of using a linking quality to find a target idea yields almost instant dividends. Note how the Pa Ingalls passage sets up "I always wondered how he could have gotten so terribly lost in such a short distance." Note also the verbal metaphor "ignorance chills me to the bone."

SYLVIE LEWIS

Snowstorm → Linking quality: *Low visibility* → Target idea: *The past*

The past is a snowstorm.

Countless crystal white days float upwards, backwards and every which way, muddling my mind with how similar they all become. Stiff, cold fingers of memory reach backwards trying to catch those snowflake days which promptly melt leaving that damp feeling that there was once something more there. Jutting up through the swirling of things past, shadowy fuzzy forms of branches, people, houses I've known and touched and held onto in warmer days. Traveling deeper into the storm, the cumbersome boots known as "How I Wish It had Been" squeak and slush, occasionally I stumble on something frozen solid. Brushing aside the gathering whiteness, there it is: a moment held firm by the ice, fossil of a feeling, colours caught, voices suspended in the circular chorus of what we said: Love's not red, it's amber and it melts all the other stuff away.

"Stiff, cold fingers of memory reach backwards trying to catch those snowflake days" uses both the expressed identity and adjective/noun versions of metaphor you've come to know and love. See how effectively they can be combined to create a startling picture of memory's struggle to reach back into the past.

Your turn. What else has *low visibility*? Find your target idea and take ten minutes to explore it through the lens of *snowstorm*. Again, remember to stay as locked into sense-bound language as you can.

Snowstorm → Linking quality: *Low visibility* → Target idea:______________

Pretty interesting, this lens thing. By the end of this challenge you'll be an expert. Brand-new glasses. Powerful magnification. Inspiring. Fun.

DAY #2

LINKING QUALITIES TO TARGET IDEAS

Prompt: Deep-Sea Diver

Here we go again. First, list three interesting qualities of a *deep-sea diver* to use as linking qualities. When you're asked to find your own linking qualities (soon), make sure they are a close relation to, e.g., *deep-sea diver's* family, that they capture an essential quality. That's the key to finding an effective *target idea*. Here they are:

Totally immersed
Supported by a lifeline
Surrounded by an unfamiliar landscape

Now, link each to a target idea—the ideas that *deep-sea diver* can be a metaphor for, by asking:

What else has that quality? What else is *totally immersed*?

As you did yesterday, take ten minutes to explore your target idea through the lens of *deep-sea diver*. Remember to stay as locked into sense-bound language as you can (e.g., a bookworm is deep-sea diving into a fantasy world).

CHARLIE WORSHAM

Deep-sea diver → Linking quality: *Totally immersed* → Target idea: *Cyclist*

A cyclist is a deep-sea diver.

His legs burn as he paddles, pushing forward with all his might. He breathes in the hard air as the world ahead of him zooms into focus from the blurry distance. The rhythmic noise of his tires spinning keeps him lost in a daydream, only this is no dream. Every twitching muscle, every ounce of energy, every brain cell, nerve, tendon, thought—it all spirals down into the abyss of the next valley. He soars upward toward the light as the world around him hangs all around, suspended almost in water. There's a coolness of wind rushing by. The whirring, stirring sounds of air fill his ears and numb his sense of the world outside. Sweat bubbles and drips from his forehead down his chest and onto the ocean bed of pavement. He is completely alone here on this road, no more above ground than a diver drifting through his world of discovery. He knows his time will run out, almost as if the air would be cut off from his lungs if he doesn't win the race. The wilderness around him is his aquarium. He is the focus, the one out of place, the pioneer in a world of sand and stone and plant and wild animal. Concentration, sharp as coral, deep in his brain as a sunken ship. The waving trees suspend time as if he swims underwater. He will not come up for air until he crosses that threshold, until the task is done. The sunlight is dampened beneath this surface of branches and leaves. His eyes do not stray, his heart beats with the deliberate intensity of a war drum. He takes in each breath like a machine. His equipment is an extension of his body. He feels the pressure pushing at him from all sides, like the kid at the bottom of the deep end seeing how long he can hold his breath. There is no outside world—there is only beating heart and smooth, liquid momentum. The nerves tingle with excitement and danger. The horizon rolls forward with him, pushed to its own edge. The winding roads dip and duck and rise and fall like the waves of clouds overhead.

What an interesting way to look at cycling. Charlie uses a nice mix of metaphor and simile to paint the picture. Take a few minutes to underline the places he submerges you.

SUSAN CATTANEO

Deep-sea diver → Linking quality: *Totally immersed* → Target idea: *In conversation*

Conversation is deep-sea diving.

Tethered to our convictions, we float out one idea after another, words dart out of our open mouths, swallowed up by the moment. Hope treads water between us, coming to rest gently on the sandy bottom, the bubble of connection, a world full of noise beyond ours, swaying, heads close …

Tethered is a close relation to *deep-sea diver.* It makes a fresh, interesting statement when applied to *convictions.*

Your turn. What else is *totally immersed*? Find your target idea and take ten minutes to explore it through the lens of *deep-sea diver.* Again, remember to stay as locked into sense-bound language as you can.

Deep-sea diver → Linking quality: *Totally immersed* → Target idea:______

Here's our second linking quality:

Deep-sea diver → Linking quality: *Supported by a lifeline* →
Target idea: ____________

Now take ten minutes to explore your new target idea through the lens of *deep-sea diver.*

TAMI NEILSEN

Deep-sea diver → Linking quality: *Supported by a lifeline* →
Target idea: *Dying patient*

The silence is loud and heavy, broken only by the distant blip of the heart-rate monitor. I am sinking under this sea of sheets and blankets, nurses and doctors circle me like sharks, watching me with cold, flat eyes, capable of giving or taking life in an instant. Surrounded by life, yet I am isolated in leagues of darkness, immersed in an ocean of hopelessness so deep, I will not return. Life is trying to escape me, trying to be done with it, but I am being force-fed life through a tube. It's not natural. Let me rip away this lifeline, this weakness. Let me instead be an anchor and sink with proud dignity.

Tami's use of first person is effective, creating a world from inside her diving suit rather than observing from the outside. Notice all the members of the diver's family she invites into the key of *dying patient.* I especially like *leagues* ...

CHARLIE WORSHAM

Deep-sea diver → Linking quality: *Supported by a lifeline* →
Target idea: *Frontline soldier*

A frontline soldier is a deep-sea diver.

> All is quiet on the frontline. The oncoming darkness is liquid in texture, not unlike the cool, murky bottom of his hometown pond, which he daydreams about when the action dies down. He listens to his watch tick away the seconds that turn to minutes that turn to hours, days, marking time till he can return to the fresh air of home. Food, water, medicine, information, all piped down to him from headquarters via a narrow, high-pressure red line on a map. One rip, one tear, and he'd be alone, surrounded by a world of enemies that know and breathe the land and air that is so strange to him. He cannot see far ahead. His helmet is hot and sticky and heavy on his head, but he mustn't remove it. His life hangs suspended in this tiny foxhole at the end of a long, narrow finger of soldiers. They are pushing into the depths. The darkness ahead holds a world of secret predators waiting to bolt from beneath a rock or dive from the blue above. He feels sluggish from exhaustion as he tries to wade through the thick air and mud that pull at his boots, his rifle, his uniform. He is drenched in sweat and filth, but immune to the smells and the sounds. Everything is soft. Softened by the long hours in battle. The supply truck comes rumbling towards him, stops. The whiting cloth of a soldier bringing his meal and ammo for the night. The silent exchange of worried glances and fingers pointing to maps that tell him what to do next. No words. Only moving parts and silent thinking. Only a thin red line keeping him connected to the outside world and survival.

See what interesting connections can be made using linking qualities? I never would have seen a soldier as a diver except for the linking phrase *supported by a lifeline*. Once you explore the question "What else has that quality?" the ideas trouble out by the wheelbarrow.

Your turn. What else is *supported by a lifeline*? Find your target idea and take ten minutes exploring it through the lens of *deep-sea diver*. Again, remember to stay as locked into sense-bound language as you can.

> Deep-sea diver → Linking quality: *Totally immersed* → Target idea:_________

Finally, try the linking phrase, *surrounded by an unfamiliar landscape*:

> Deep-sea diver → Linking quality: *Surrounded by an unfamiliar landscape* →
> Target idea: ______________:

SUSAN CATTANEO

Deep-sea diver → Linking quality: *Surrounded by an unfamiliar landscape* → Target idea: *Astronaut on the moon*

An astronaut on the moon is a deep-sea diver.

Stars floating in a black sea, kicking up slow-motion dust, the noisy intake of air, slow motion arms paddling through the dense air, your skin saran wrapped in white puffy material, feet grasping for purchase on the rocky bottom, the cocoon of silence outside your glass mask …

Many family members and many notes in each key are shared by the diver and the astronaut. But to see the universe of stars as "floating in a black sea" is pretty special, once again brought to you by your friendly sponsor, the diver's linking term, *surrounded by an unfamiliar landscape.*

CHANELLE DAVIS

Deep-sea diver → Linking quality: *Surrounded by an unfamiliar landscape* → Target idea: *Tourist*

Tourist is a deep-sea diver.

Submerged in crowds of people with unfamiliar accents, beautiful slim woman gliding along the city streets covered in treasures, diving in and out of cafés, high buildings with shimmering windows, speeding on the subway through dark echoing tunnels, shimmering flashes of colour from massive billboards like coral reefs, rushing around with my camera trying to capture beautiful statues under jellyfish clouds suspended in the sky.

I've never looked at a city like this before. Fresh and interesting. I love "jellyfish clouds suspended in the sky." Thanks, Chanelle.

Your turn. What else is *surrounded by an unfamiliar landscape*? Find your target idea and take ten minutes to explore it through the lens of *deep-sea diver.* Again, remember to stay as locked into sense-bound language as you can.

Deep-sea diver → Linking quality: *Surrounded by an unfamiliar landscape* → Target idea:______________

DAY #3

LINKING QUALITIES TO TARGET IDEAS

Prompt: Guitar Solo

Once again, you'll go through the process. It's a pretty healthy exercise, and it really tones your writing muscles. Tomorrow you'll take this exercise another step further, but for now, use three qualities of a guitar solo as your linking qualities. Try these:

Building intensity
Going somewhere new
In the spotlight

Now link each quality to a target idea—the ideas that *guitar solo* can be a metaphor for, by asking:

What else has that quality? What else is *building intensity?*

Take ten minutes to explore your target idea through the lens of *guitar solo*.

CHANELLE DAVIS

Guitar solo → Linking quality: *Building intensity* → Target idea: *River*

A river is a guitar solo.

Water swelling up, building momentum as it flows, bending through the landscape, accelerating, rising in rapids, creating tension against the rocks, reaching its highest pitch as an audience of trees sway in adoration, the river descends down the rock face …

If you didn't know the prompt, Chanelle's writing would be a pretty exciting look at a river, with subtle members of the river and guitar families sharing "bending." I've never seen trees (swaying) at a rock concert before, but I guess there are plenty of rocks to go around. Nice.

CHARLIE WORSHAM

Guitar solo → Linking quality: *Building intensity* →
Target idea: *Lawyer's closing argument*

A lawyer's closing argument is a guitar solo.

He rises with silent determination and strides forward into the spotlight of the packed courtroom. The crowd holds its breath, knowing that this will be the moment they take home that night and replay in stories and in dreams over and over and over. He turns to face the jury with a nervous swagger, lifts his arms, and begins to speak. The first few words are calm and spaced with even phrasing, even tone, and simple inflection. You can see the faces on the front row nod to the rhythm, pick up the theme. Louder now, his words echo across the room, masterfully driven toward each pair of captive ears. He explores the stage in front of the judge's bench, the fervor and intensity building as his plea grows more desperate. He drips sweat from his brow, his collar tearing loose as his body moves to the wordplay, arms pointing and diving to exaggerate the message and drive it home. He draws in every last ounce of energy in that room, held silence in his palm for a moment, and with the outpouring of a sudden thunderstorm, lets the last sentence land onto the polished wood floor like a guitar crushed and burning, screaming and wailing through a humming tube amp. The crowd erupts into a frenzy, the drumming gavel of the judge comes down again and again. He moves over to the waiting wings of associate lawyers, sits down, and bows his head, completely spent.

Yikes! Jimmy Page, move over! I love how the linking qualities lead to such interesting places. You can do it easily, too, step by step. Go ahead.

What else *builds intensity*? Find your target idea and take ten minutes to explore it through the lens of *guitar solo*. Again, remember to stay as locked into sense-bound language as you can.

Guitar solo → Linking quality: *Building intensity* → Target idea:___________

Next, *Going somewhere new.* Write for ten minutes.

GREG BECKER

Guitar solo → Linking quality: *Going somewhere new* → Target idea: *First date*

A first date is a guitar solo.

His heart races as he stands on the stage of her porch and his blood starts pumping louder. His fingers curl into a fist and he raps his knuckles on her door to the beat of his thumping heart which he can feel all the way to his feet. The surrounding world vanishes as the door opens he feels naked in the spotlight of the overhanging porch light and the sounds of the evening are silenced as she reaches out for his hand from the darkness. The evening is a three hour crescendo a with all words, jokes, quick glances and touches leading to the final ten seconds where their lips finally consummate the relationship and a new light is sparked and lifted from the crowd of lovers across the dark night landscape.

Not only does this create an interesting picture of a first date, it also creates an interesting picture of a guitar solo. As you'll see tomorrow, sometimes it's good to go both ways. I love the porch light as a spotlight.

CHARLIE WORSHAM

Guitar solo → Linking quality: *Going somewhere new* →
Target idea: *Piloting an airplane*

Piloting an airplane is a guitar solo.

Strapped in, waiting for our chance to take off, we roll across the stage of airplanes and personnel standing on the tarmac. Once I get the nod to take the main runway, we can feel the momentum build as the main engine kicks into high gear. Picking up speed, I feel the wheels leave the ground—the rush of being suspended in midair. Thrust upward, watching the night sky engulf me as the twinkling lights of the city below flicker like lighters and cell phones in a crowded arena. The great, powerful rumble of the jet surrounds me, yet in my hand I hold the keys to a new frontier. A throttle and steering mechanism—my instruments of choice—to lead me to places I've never been. I know where I will land; I do not know exactly how I will get there, soaring above the clouds and across a vast ocean below. I will roll onward post-landing, waiting for my next chance to take off, reflect the glow of a moon spotlight, dance among the stars, swoop and dive through the air. Each minute adjustment of my fingers and hands result in giant sweeps of movement that reverberate for miles and can be seen and felt by all in its wake. The cockpit, like my brain right now, locked safely from the surrounding chaos and noise, it is here I will steer the arc of my flight, my half composed, half fate-driven solo beneath the stars.

Looking at an object through a lens of another thing can transform and enlarge that object, as shown here. Charlie's description of the flight wouldn't be as focused without the lens of *guitar solo*. It allows the flight to become something fresh and new, something recognized and not recognized at the same time. Lenses.

Your turn. What else *goes somewhere new*? Find your target idea and take ten minutes to explore it through the lens of *guitar solo*. Again, remember to stay as locked into sense-bound language as you can.

Guitar solo → Linking quality: *Going somewhere new* →
Target idea:_________

Finally, *in the spotlight*.

Guitar solo → Linking quality: *In the spotlight* → Target idea: _____________

For ten minutes explore your target idea through the lens of *guitar solo*.

MEGAN BURTT

Guitar solo → Linking quality: *In the spotlight* → Target idea: *Moth*

A moth's guitar solo

Fluttering aimlessly about, starving for attention, the moth soldiers on, desperate to find home in a bright ray. Little does the bugger know that once you find the light, there is no turning back. Caught in the shine, he is weighing distraction, which may lend itself to death by design and excitement. Finding the radiant torch bigger than its delicate body can handle, the moth takes its last little moth breath morsel and plummets down, its quest stopped it dead in its tracks. But the light remains, waiting for its next victim.

Wow! Tough spotlight. The linking quality sees all the fallen guitar heroes who shone for a moment, then were torched by their quest for the light. I'll never see spotlights in the same way again. That's the power of metaphor.

GREG BECKER

Guitar solo → Linking quality: *In the spotlight* → Target idea: *Escaping convict*

An escaping convict guitar solo

He strums the bars of his cage with his metal cup giving the signal to the others that the moment has arrived and he is ready. Slowly the row of cells quiets and the prison goes silent except for rhythmic thumping of his heart and the small scratching and clicking of his makeshift key unlocking his door. Once he steps out of his cell and the door swings open, the cell block erupts in cheers and yells as he makes his mad dash for the exit door. A wandering spotlight catches his foot and quickly locks onto him as he darts back and forth across the prison yard.

Apparently, neither Megan nor Greg see spotlights as a positive thing. I love "strums the bars of his cage" and "rhythmic thumping of his heart."

Your turn. What else is in the spotlight? Find your target idea and take ten minutes to explore it through the lens of *guitar solo*. Again, remember to stay as locked into sense-bound language as you can.

Guitar solo → Linking quality: *In the spotlight* → Target idea:_______________

DAY #4

WORKING BOTH DIRECTIONS

Prompt: Sleeping Late

You've had plenty of practice exploring one idea through the lens of another idea. Using linking qualities, it's an effective and efficient way to see one thing as though it were something else—the definition of metaphor. Ready to try something new today?

As usual, you'll link each to a target idea—the ideas that *sleeping late* can be a metaphor for, by asking:

What else has that quality?

So far, you've been looking at the target idea (arrived at via the linking quality) through the lens of the first idea (in this case, *sleeping late).* Today, you'll do something else, too.

As an example, say that your linking quality from *sleeping late* is *feeling lazy.* The target idea could be *avoiding your homework:*

Sleeping late → Feeling lazy → *Avoiding your homework*

So, as usual, you look at *avoiding your homework* through the lens of *sleeping late.* Like this:

> Equations, scraggly bits of ink blotting the page, beeping at me, an alarm clock nudging me to clear the haze from my brain and crawl over to the chair, bend my back, and start scratching solutions in the waiting white blanks. My brain hits its snooze button, rolling over into visions of clear mountain streams bubbling past smooth white stones, speckled trout darting in the shallows unaware of the slow motion line about to drop a blue winged fly, plop, on the wrinkling surface … buzz, buzz from the equal sign, opening like a mouth while I squeeze my eyes shut.

But now you'll spend another ten minutes reversing directions: After you finish your first ten minutes writing about *avoiding your homework* through the lens of *sleeping late,* you'll change directions and look at *sleeping late* through the lens of *avoiding your homework.* Like this:

> Rolling over, sinking into the soft white pillow, echoes of Miss Luger's shrill chirp, long miles of polished hallways ago, burrowing through the haze, the nudging elbow of a conscience needling me with visions of algebra problems waiting with raised eyebrows, or the Battle of Gettysburg whining for a date to begin the fray. I snuggle into my blank white sheet and relax my shoulders, drifting away from old piled workbooks at the corner of my desk to sunny afternoons with no alarm clock

voices calling from the old Sunday nights before homework was due at St. Peter's grammar school.

Now, try this. Supply the target idea for each of the linking qualities below:

Conserving energy
Wasting time

First use *conserving energy* as your linking quality. As usual, when you find your target idea, take ten minutes to explore your target idea through the lens of *sleeping late.*

Sleeping late → Linking quality: *Conserving energy* →
Target idea: *Sitting on a summer porch*

Sitting on a summer porch is like sleeping late.

The heat of the day slows down the world, a slow molasses wind stubbornly blows across the porch having no effect at all. The heavy blanket of August weighs you down until you are motionless listening to the buzzing of the cicadas, thinking about moving, thinking about something cold to drink, thinking about the day ahead but acting on nothing. Eyes are droopy and won't open any time soon. The world walks by on slow motion somehow all moving on with their days, walking, talking, going somewhere. This is as far as you go, even to stand would require the entire reserve of energy left in your bones.

Now reverse it and explore *sleeping late* through the lens of your target idea for ten minutes.

Sleeping late is sitting on a summer porch.

The dream scape lays out before you just over the railing of wakefulness. You still have a clear image of the world of fantasy that you were just in moments ago as it slowly pulls away you cling to every last detail in your memory. The dream soon becomes just another neighbor walking their surreality by your brain coming into view and then gone. Your legs squirm and wander beneath the sheets in search of the shady cool spots, re-energizing the weight of sleep once found. These final five minutes of snooze are but an illusion of security, of comfort and safety. The day is just moments away from overtaking you, and the frail wood railing of reality weakens the more it is leaned upon.

Wonderful how this changes directions so easily. I love "The heavy blanket of August weighs you down," and, going the other direction, "the railing of wakefulness." See how the metaphor can make a U-turn and head back the other way, too.

CHARLIE WORSHAM

Sleeping late → Linking quality: *Conserving energy* →
Target idea: *Taking the bus instead of walking*

Taking the bus instead of walking is like sleeping late.

Exhausted, spent, I yawn my way onto the rumbling bus, warm and blanketed from the cold outside. I curl into the first open seat, tangled in my many layers of clothing. I shield the daylight from my eyes with my arm and squeeze in a few more minutes of drooling, dozing half-consciousness. Anything to avoid the moment that my legs will get a mind of their own, leading the charge into alertness and wide awake at the end of the route. In my mind, I'm punching the snooze button every time the bell rings to signal another stop along the way. My brain rattles on a few times. False starts like an old engine too cranky to keep its gears moving just yet. Five more minutes till I have to pull my face from the cool glass pillow I'm leaning against, crawl out of this cozy hard plastic bed, and step onto the sidewalk. The outside world buzzes and bounces around me, too much light and color and sound to take in at once. I squint and rub my eyes and stretch my back and arms and stumble into the day.

"Warm and blanketed" sets up this bus ride, bringing in important members of *sleeping late*'s family. "Yawn" helps out, too. Then other family members ring the buzzer to get in. Nice.

Now reverse it and explore *sleeping late* through the lens of your target idea for ten minutes.

Sleeping late is like taking the bus instead of walking.

The alarm clock screeches— like the squeal of rusty brakes in my ears pulling me against my will out of the dark cave of deep sleep. My thoughts, smiles, to-dos, are all lining up just outside the door of my brain, waiting for the morning commute inbound. They stand sleepily, or sit in a daze on sidewalk benches, mindless daydreamers reading the paper, playing games on their phones. A bus comes hurtling towards the stop, brakes hissing loudly jolting some awake as they march onto the platform. In my half-wake, half-dream, I feel these thoughts begin to stir. My leg slides over to a fresh, cool spot on the mattress, I become aware of the glow behind the curtain. The bus runs without me, but I can rest my eyes in a backseat while someone else drives. I can skate through the journey to awake effortlessly, rocking to the drone of the wheels and the heavy air vent and the windshield wipers and the periodic bells marking our arrival at each stop along the way. I don't have to grab the wheel. I don't burn the gas. I save it for when I really need it. The last minute. It's actually a complex ritual—alarm one, alarm two, I throw the covers off for a minute, I halfway sit up with eyes closed. I stand in the shower under hot running water. I lift the heaviness of sleep off my shoulders and eyes one brick at a time. Why burn that energy if it can just roll off my back of its own accord?

I like how Charlie turns his thoughts into commuters: "My thoughts, smiles, to-dos, are all lining up just outside the door of my brain, waiting for the morning commute inbound." Marvelous!

Your turn. Using *conserving energy* as your linking quality, find your target idea and take ten minutes to explore it through the lens of *sleeping late*.

Then reverse it and explore *sleeping late* through the lens of your target idea for ten minutes.

Now try *wasting time* as your linking quality. As usual, when you find your target idea, take ten minutes to explore your target idea through the lens of *sleeping late*. Then reverse it and explore *sleeping late* through the lens of your target idea for ten minutes.

SUSAN CATTANEO

Sleeping late → Linking quality: *Wasting time* → Target idea: *Surfing the Web*

Sleeping late as surfing the Web

Eyes glazed over with sleep, the late morning sun powering up, sheets wrapped like cords around my body, keyboard pattern of sunlight through the squares of the window, the hum of the traffic outside the window, the soft whir of the alarm clock, dreams run on the flat screen of my mind, fingers of memory scrolling through images, there I am at six, standing up my knees in a mud puddle behind our house, a grin as wide as a pumpkin's on my face, my curls are a tangled mess of bits and bytes, brain clicks "like" …

Surfing the Web as sleeping late

Hands lie over the keyboard, curled on the couch, dazed and catatonic in the blue light of the screen, my slumbering mind moves from page to page, the hours pass like a dream, lazy thoughts come and go, "I should get to bed" surfaces for a moment, but the pull of the Web drags me back down, the laptop rests on the tops of my thighs, heat emanating from its metal skin like a lover's touch, like an electric blanket …

The two families intermingle, each making visits to the other's house. *Surfing the Web's* family brings *powering up, cords, keyboard pattern, hum, whir, flat screen, scrolling, bits and bytes, and clicks and like* to the party. Quite a roomful.

Sleeping late's family returns the favor, bringing *BBQ and beer,* as well as an *electric blanket*. Nice, folks.

KEPPIE COUTTS

Sleeping late → Linking quality: *Wasting time* →
Target idea: *A dead-end relationship*

A dead-end relationship as sleeping late

I know that I should wake up from this fog, wipe the crust and crumbs from my eyes, and see this for what is really is. But there is a weight, like the warm blanket of blood-red darkness in sleep that keeps me in this myopia, hoping for some revelation like daylight to break through the curtains of dysfunction, and even when I know that your eyes stray, there is the same paralysis of late morning mangled-up dreams, where the mind knows one thing to be true, but the body simply refuses to move.

Reverse it and explore *sleeping late* through the lens of your target idea for ten minutes.

Sleeping late as a dead-end relationship

Warm throbs of sleep like waves on the movie screens of my eyelids; waves that seem to touch my face, cajole me into staying where I am, like a lover's hands touching my shoulders and rounding to the back of my neck just as I'm about to walk out the door. Things to do, groceries to buy, money to be made, life to be lived, and yet I stay in a shallow seduction. Every extra minute under the bedsheets, head buried in the chest of a pillow, starts to gather the dust of guilt, which compounds the problem, adds extra weight, keeps you there longer ... Guilt sprouts tentacles that tangle and wrap, entwine and twist like vines, until you find yourself enmeshed in the very thing that is dragging you down ...

Simile is very useful here: "like the warm blanket," "like a lover's hands," and "twist like vines." As usual, it lets you mention something without committing to it. Plenty of family visiting here.

Your turn. Using *wasting time* as your linking quality, find your target idea and take ten minutes to explore it through the lens of *sleeping late.*

Then reverse it and explore *sleeping late* through the lens of your target idea for minutes.

DAY #5

WORKING BOTH DIRECTIONS

Prompt: Broken Glass

Being able to reverse directions—to move in either direction through the linking quality—requires a linking quality that is an essential feature of your first idea. You'll see more of this process today.

First, list two interesting qualities of *broken glass*:

Unable to be repaired
Glittering and dangerous

Link each to a target idea—the ideas that *broken glass* can be a metaphor for:

What else has that quality? What else is *unable to be repaired?*

Now, try this. Supply the target idea for each of the linking qualities. Like yesterday, after you finish your first ten minutes writing about your target idea through the lens of *broken glass,* you'll change directions and look at *broken glass* through the lens of your target idea.

First, work with *unable to be repaired.*

CHARLIE WORSHAM

Broken glass → Linking quality: *Unable to be repaired* →
Target idea: *Broken trust*

Broken trust is broken glass.

I watch her words crash through me. Everything I believe in cracks and shatters and lies around me in a pool of silvery shards. I can't begin to try to pick up the pieces and put them back together. Every time I reach out to her and try to trust again, I feel sharp edges tear into the fingers of my heart. My mind tells me to get a broom and dustpan and just sweep up what's left of our relationship and dump it into the trash. Trust forms in the heat of a great fire, and the complex melted elements that make up its fragile and beautiful structure are one of a kind every time. Once trust shatters, it destroys all fingerprints. And no tunesmith in the world can mend a break like that.

A very effective expressed identity, "trust is glass," both in forming and breaking it. It works well, seeing broken trust as broken glass. I love, "Once trust shatters, it destroys all fingerprints." Read on to see how Charlie turns it around.

Reverse it and explore *broken glass* through the lens of your target idea for ten minutes.

Broken glass is like broken trust.

The screeching tires, the horns screaming wildly, the quick vacuum of air before the thundering impact. The explosion of metal and plastic and rubber and glass thrown into the air and raining down like so many tinkling notes on a toy piano.

There lies the bed of clear blue shards on gooey summer pavement. Each dagger of light-catching glass crunches under foot. The driver emerges from the dented, bent-in door, staggers his way to the curb. He might as well have cried tragic confetti instead of the watery tears. That broken glass is the picture of his next four years. Sixteen, a new license, a handshake and a knowing look from father. The pieces of windshield that stick to his shoe and carpet the road will stick with him for who knows how long. He won't be allowed the chance to avoid this again. The new car will go away, totaled. Any new vehicle will be a shadow of this one. Keys will be like rations of daylight handed to a solitarily confined prisoner for good behavior. What's broken is broken and lies irreparable, reflecting in jagged fractions of a portrait the sad face of one who has lost his freedom.

The shattering of glass leads to the boy's losing his father's trust after a car accident. Charlie puts them together nicely in "The pieces of windshield that stick to his shoe and carpet the road will stick with him for who knows how long."

SUSAN CATTANEO

Broken glass → Linking quality: *Unable to be repaired* →
Target idea: *Mental illness*

Mental illness as broken glass

You lie on the metal bed, wrists and ankles bound in leather straps that cut into your skin, eyes listless and infocused, the doctor stands above you, speaking in soft tones but you only hear shards of his conversation, your thoughts shatter at every word, reflecting a thousand ideas all at once, sharp memories jab you, demanding attention. Your sanity is a cracked window, and you need to see beyond it. This time will be different. This time, there is something to see once you get past the glass. So, you raise a hard boot and feel the delightful sound of your heel on the smooth surface, the swift kick and the tiny fairy wing sound of all those pieces, but there's only darkness beyond and you.

Look at all the members of *broken glass*'s family are introduced to *mental illness*. Nice motion in this direction. Now Susan turns it around:

Broken glass as mental illness

The window's shards lie in a catatonic state on the floor, dazed from the feeling of being whole one moment and then shattered the next. Each splinter of glass is crazy sharp, reflecting a thousand distorted images of the same blue sky, a reality only seen in tiny pieces, the cracked wooden frame holds desperately onto a few brittle triangles, a straightjacket of peeling white paint clinging onto these last fragile scraps, but the wood is rotten and the aged white hands slowly surrender the final pieces, they tumble, falling head over heel onto the dark cold pavement.

Susan personifies the glass, especially effective in "Each splinter of glass is crazy sharp, reflecting a thousand distorted images of the same blue sky, a reality only seen in tiny pieces." If the linking quality is essential enough to the original idea, the target idea will be more likely to turn around easily, since they'll share many family members. The fewer qualities they share, the more likely simile becomes.

Your turn. Using *unable to be repaired* as your linking quality, find your target idea and take ten minutes to explore it through the lens of *broken glass.*

Now reverse it and explore *sleeping late* through the lens of your target idea for ten minutes.

How about *glittering and dangerous* as a linking quality?

JESS MEIDER

Broken glass → Linking quality: *Glittering and dangerous* → Target idea: *Las Vegas*

Las Vegas as broken glass

Night flight over darkness, heavy feeling in body resounding as plane descends, the disco ball oasis sitting up ahead he spies it … glittering city of lights like a wondrous song of glass and metal tinkles in the quiet of his mind. Sharpened desires, cold diamond like yen sparkle, each flashing light a hardened prayer of someone eyes glassed over, greedy, hope transformed into the heavy wishes for change, the money fairy, god, angel, lady luck, all looming above like grey ghouls smiling over the lit city. Birdseye, ominous, regal, palatial city. Landed, he is just another speck gathering to worship cash, like a delusional disciple. The glitterlike ice he snorts up his nose; it embodies and possesses him shards and shrapnel, solidifying into one big crystal ball, fortune and fame visually stunning, he rolls his bets all his money on 7, BAH, nope, rolling crystal ball tips over the edge of fancy skyscraper, soaring towards the gravity below, past the neon flashing lights towards the shattering future.

Seeing a city as broken glass is pretty interesting. Possible, of course, only through the action of a strong linking quality like *glittering and dangerous*. I like how Jess turns the narrator into a piece of broken glass, "landed, he is just another speck gathering to worship cash."

Broken glass is a Las Vegas of light.

Three million glittering eyes, each heart a sliver of a whole, the belief that there is better beyond the next bet. Shards lined like hotels and gambling houses, flat, round, ridged on the edges, the trip that is glassy, fragile and extremely brittle, dry like a desert that heats up and cools down every day, fantastic dazzle, a beautiful show musical big booming orchestras overtones of Frank Sinatra echoing thru the night, the midnight players pounding and smashing hearts every night, all these fabricated lights glitter like shards of people's hopes, a disco ball, inviting the next gullible sucker.

Look at all the family members lining up for the buffet. I love that both the inhabitants and the buildings become shards of broken glass. Great turnaround.

CHARLIE WORSHAM

Broken glass → Linking quality: *Glittering and dangerous* →
Target idea: *Beautiful stranger*

A beautiful stranger is broken glass.

There she is, a shining mess of broken heart pieces wrapped in a lace dress and diamonds, poised at the bar with a crystal glass to her lips. Every eye in the room is pulled to her like sailors to a siren song. It's a sexy kind of pain. To break the skin and feel the thrill as the blood draws to the surface. Her breath frosts the window, her voice could shatter a pyramid of wineglasses. She catches the light and catches the attention of a particularly dreamy-eyed fellow. She keeps the edges hidden behind red lipstick and sweet perfume, a painted predator. He's helpless as a kid who busts out the window and has to test the jagged edge of the cracked pane with his finger.

Wow, how do you get from *broken glass* to *beautiful stranger?* You know the answer: "What else has that quality?" Charlie paints a fresh, interesting picture.

Broken glass is a beautiful stranger.

I knew I was losing my grip about halfway down the stairs. It was one of those slow-motion moments when you know you could stop the disaster but you know you're gonna miss your shot. There it goes, the mirror I stood in front of every morning for the past three years, flying down the stairwell so gracefully and silent, only to explode on the concrete like a grenade slamming shrapnel in every direction. I held my breath and watched a million-piece orchestra strike its every note at once. A fireworks display of crystal reflecting the fluorescent lights, metal rails, my red T-shirt, my white skin and mouth open wide in wonder. And as soon as it began it was over. The ghost of an elusive stranger, one I stood before every morning for three years but never spoke to. Except to tell it about me—my problems, my joys, my practice sessions for what I might say to a pretty girl or a disappointed teacher. I never thought about how much I trusted that old thing. It held my darkest secrets, my most private moments. It knew my weaknesses more than my parents or best friend. And I trusted it not to tell. How dangerous—if that mirror could talk, what it could say!

Very cool, using the mirror to reflect back onto himself as the stranger. It may be a bit of a stretch but still a fresh and interesting place to look.

Your turn. Using *glittering and dangerous* as your linking quality, find your target idea and take ten minutes to explore it through the lens of *broken glass*.

Now reverse it and explore *broken glass* through the lens of your target idea for ten minutes.

DAY #6

WORKING BOTH DIRECTIONS

Prompt: Falling in Love

Finding ideas that can easily turn around is a great tool, and like any tool, all it takes is practice. So keep practicing.

First list two interesting qualities of *falling in love:*

> Swept away
> Glittering and dangerous

Now link each to a target idea—the ideas that *falling in love* can be a metaphor for, by asking:

What else has that quality? What else is *swept away?*

Try this. Supply the target idea for each of the linking qualities. As you did yesterday, after you finish your first ten minutes, you'll spend another ten minutes reversing directions.

It starts with *swept away:*

SUSAN

Falling in love → Linking quality: *Swept away* → Target idea: *Hurricane*

A hurricane as falling in love

Clouds hug the darkening summer night, branches dance and sway, lightning pulses, a heartbeat in the chest of the open sky, nature closes its eyes, welcoming the rush of power, tingling in the fingertips of trees and the dark hair of thunder-clouds, dark earth opens its parched lips to the kissing rain, raindrops coat and dance in the darkness, streetlights blink demurely, giddy trees tilt and bend in the wind, a roof peels up off a house, shedding its tiles with abandon, river water swells its banks, sensuously caressing the stone bridge, cars come to a standstill, their headlights are a pearl necklace glittering …

I've never been this attracted to a hurricane. What an interesting look Susan provides here. Notice the stacking of metaphors in "branches dance and sway, lightning pulses, a heartbeat in the chest of the open sky." Wow.

Falling in love is a hurricane.

Wrapped in a cloud of sheets, desire pours like rain from my body, a lightning flash pulling me into the eye of the storm, your gentle words tumble and sway in front of me, my heart zaps with electric charge when I feel you near, passion blows through me, tearing at my senses, your clothes, the delicate hush of your kiss is the eye, then being drenched in pounding thunder …

Again, lots of shared family members here, a tribute to the power of a strong linking quality.

SCARLET KEYS

Falling in love → Linking quality: *Swept away* → Target idea: *Flash flood*

Flash flood as falling in love

It comes out of nowhere, the silent emptiness and then the downpour. Thunder like fireworks, lightning laughter, surrender to the force of it; fear submerges and you float, legs and arms out, on the top of unexpected whirl. You, there on the yellow plastic raft, drink in hand with your little paper umbrella taking in the sun, then water holds you like midnight arms you move with the random flow, until you are spinning, tornado. Tears funnel and swell, you are circling the drain you are holding your breath fetal and stunned. You wished for rain, something to revive and soften your thirsty heart and it stormed and it stole from you, but you can die from too much rain. Your wish didn't have a boundary or a shape, you smelled the empty dust and then you choked from the raging force that found you a sad autumn leaf and left you washed away stuck on the side of the road too drenched to dance and blow down the sidewalk …

Of course, the other direction seems easier. Scarlet does an effective job in this direction, wishing for rain and getting swept away. I'd never seen a flash flood from this perspective, and it was only possible through the linking quality.

Falling in love is a flash flood.

You flashed your lightning smile and that was it, I was the hostage of your every move, the thrill of suddenness, breathless and drenched in the overwhelming feeling of the swell. Floating and shivering wide awake in the awe of it. Kissing kissing like little knives of rain up and down my body, buckling under the force of you, skin wet and warm, it's a heart with no life jacket, it's running in the dark, it's a rush when it happens out of nowhere like it does rising up around me I am saturated and exhausted, it's all I think about pulse rushing and scrambling like it's blindfolded in a labyrinth, in the breathless spin, the feeling as if all the air was being sucked out of the room at once and you are alive with the moment standing on a cliff, your head in grey heavy clouds, the taste of metal, the taste of bliss and fear like holding a gun encased in cashmere, your eyes closed, your heart hoping that when it all settles and quiets and the s ...

This direction is easier, but look at Scarlet's simile, "kissing kissing like little knives of rain up and down my body, buckling under the force of you." It still results in a fresh, interesting look at falling in love. Nice.

Your turn. Using *swept away* as your linking quality, find your target idea and take ten minutes to explore it through the lens of *falling in love*.

Now reverse it and explore *falling in love* through the lens of your target idea for ten minutes.

Here we go with *glittering and dangerous:*

CAROLINE HARVEY

Falling in love → Linking quality: *Glittering and dangerous* →
Target idea: *Las Vegas*

Las Vegas as falling in love

You plunge into it as fast as your wheels will roll you, hurrying to dive into the sparkling chaos, to sink your teeth into the fertile promise of abundance and all that tempting wealth. Your desire to stake your claim, to plant your flag, to be the underworld king in this wild arena of hustlers and go-go dancers shakes you crazy and loose like a flower clinging to the roadside in a windstorm. Your need to win at this gambler's game that rides up your back like a bucking horse; you're at the mercy of this beast of compulsion. Inside, once you've penetrated the deep inner world and can see the shimmer of lights, taste the pump of fresh oxygen coming in through the secret holes in velvet walls, you slide like a slick snake up to the blackjack table, you lay your golden goods out for all to see, you bet more than you should because you just feel lucky, a single line of sweat forms across your chest as you hold steady and silently beg god to give you one good, sweet surge of victory before it ends.

Yikes! What a sexy view of Las Vegas, the great temptress. Hot spot: "go-go dancers shakes you crazy and loose like a flower clinging to the roadside in a windstorm."

Falling in love as Las Vegas

It is dawn, it is desert quiet and windless, you are standing just outside the bedroom door. You are inhaling, seizing as much air into your hungry, electric body as you can. Everything in you is preparing for the shock-white neon beam of lightning on the other side of the door, the promise of frenzied, chaotic, rich victory that's about to bloom up over a mountain of bedsheets and explode you. You know, once you nod your head subtly up and then down, indicate the universal symbol of yes, yes, please, hit me again, you know there won't be any turning back. You'll have the best intentions, you'll tell yourself you'll only hand over half of your heart, you'll only saddle up to the high roller table for a little while, only show a few of cards and keep the rest tight to your trapdoor chest. But you won't be able to stop yourself.

Beautiful turnaround. Note the many Las Vegas family members Caroline invites into the bedroom. Again, a tribute to a strong linking quality, providing your quest for great metaphor with a smooth roadway through the dry desert of infertile options.

SUSAN CATTANEO

Falling in love → Linking quality: *Glittering and dangerous* → Target idea: *Dagger*

Dagger as falling in love

Longing smooth metal, shining warm in the light from a candle, velvet drapes hanging from stone walls, long blond hair tied back with a simple ribbon, breath rising softly from the delicately laced chest, bending over her, hand on the jeweled

> handle, hand caresses the metal, pulling the blade from the sheath with a gentle movement, the sigh of metal leaving leather, the blade shivering close to the skin, the tiny pinprick making a drop of ruby precious blood, sharp double edge whispering, longing to break the skin open, to sink deeply into muscle and bone, hard metal meeting soft flesh, the blade melting and blood pouring from the wound, warm and welcome, absolution, the sweet smell of perfume and revenge,

Personified in its longing, the dagger drips lust and danger. Scary stuff, brought to you by your friendly sponsor, *glittering and dangerous.*

> *Falling in love is a dagger.*
>
> The sweet warm metal of your words, slicing through any and all my defenses, glinting in your light, I am drawn in by my own reflection, my heart is encrusted with precious stones, ruby for passion, emerald for jealousy, the blade sings to me, beckons to come closer, to reach out a delicate finger and run it against the honed edge, I intake sharply as I am pierced, pinned to this love, a butterfly, delicate wings open and lain down on white linen, exposed, a specimen on your wall, caught between your fingertips in the dusk of one summer evening, my colors vibrant and preserved …

I love the secondary expressed identity, "I am pierced, pinned to this love, a butterfly, delicate wings open … ."

Your turn. Using *glittering and dangerous* as your linking quality, find your target idea and take ten minutes to explore it through the lens of *falling in love.*

Now reverse it and explore *falling in love* through the lens of your target idea for ten minutes.

DAY #7

WORKING BOTH DIRECTIONS

Prompt: Cheating Lover

This will be the last day of working an idea both ways, and as usual, I will supply the linking qualities. The ability to go deep enough into your idea to find an *essential* linking quality will accelerate your search for effective metaphor.

First, list two interesting qualities of *cheating lover:*

Swept away
Dangerous situation

Now link each to a target idea—the ideas that *cheating lover* can be a metaphor for, by asking:

What else has that quality?

SCARLET KEYS

Cheating lover → *Swept away* → Target idea: *Avalanche*

An avalanche is a cheating lover.

You shake the ground burying everything in your path alive. Icy fingers wipe away all that is sacred, like it was lint on your lover's coat. You have no allegiance; you live for the rush without stopping to think about the wreckage of the aftermath. The lives left breathless, the naked earth that breathes like the dying deer on the side of the road. I watch you slip and slide through shadows and sunlight, around corners and valleys finally to end up in a pile of cold wreckage. You come without a warning; you end with your frosted breath still frigid and more alive for it. You have had the thrill of the rush, I watch and mourn for all that is in your path. The smell of the burn of whirling out of control, the feeling of the ground like a midnight train rumbling and pushing through a sleeping town, clouds hover and twist …

Note Scarlet's use of direct address, talking directly to the avalanche as though it were a person. Very effective. Again, an effective mingling of the families of both ideas.

A cheating lover is an avalanche.

The unexpected shake in the ground, the feel of a cold sliding beneath my solid feet. I fall, blinded by the blur of heated deceit, covered in disbelief, isolated and suffocated by the choices you've made, unstoppable. I am buried alive by grief. When did you first brush up against one another, when did the first quiver or rush just beneath your restless skin begin? The rumbles of what was to come, the moment you collided and the first crack in my trust waited to burst and rupture? The sight of it all is still stuck in my throat, frozen words, shards of crystalized pain that stab and puncture, splinters of the life before and the life after the collapse of the life I'd known. Breathing is slow and cold, Lamaze, blinking back tears, stunned, swallowed in the aftermath, trying to fini ...

Direct address again, this time to the cheating lover, "when did the first quiver or rush just beneath your restless skin begin?" Scarlet uses the *avalanche* family to drive home how much damage the lover has done. Great turnaround.

PAT PATTISON

Cheating lover → *Swept away* → Target idea: *Waterfall*

A waterfall is a cheating lover

Murmuring, then plunging over the edge, splashing off rocks slippery, ducking and hiding, in a flash of sunlight, revealing secret places, flotsam from upstream, fool's gold glittering at the bottom, calling like a lover, dive in, take me up in your hands, cold and dripping. The wind curls and slides, wrapping in mist, cascading to the bottom, foaming like a lace petticoat dropped to the floor, chilling me, warning me away. Whispers of mist dancing, like smoke in a bar, the throbbing of rhythms pounding to the depths, power like a punch ...

A cheating lover is a waterfall.

I hear the pounding, insistent, cascading down the stairs, splashing my face like cold water, a power punch to my body, I'm caught in a current pulling, dragging me downward. I'm tumbling, upside down, swept over the edge into the chasm, breathless: breathe! My lungs screaming for air, my heart the size of a basketball, skydiver in the middle of an endless fall to the bottom, a pool of silence. Voices whispering, wet tongues slurring sweaty promises to the dark, the twisted bedspread. Fog rising in my brain. I'm weak and drowning. Lying in a pool that ...

Your turn. Using *swept away* as your linking quality, find your target idea and take ten minutes to explore it through the lens of *cheating lover.*

Now reverse it and explore *cheating lover* through the lens of your target idea for ten minutes.

Now, here's a shot at *dangerous situation*. The danger could be to the cheater, risking retribution. The danger could be to the cheated, losing love. A lot of places to go.

STAN SWINIARSKI

Cheating lover → *Dangerous situation* →
Target idea: *Kids playing with a loaded gun*

Kids playing with a loaded gun are like cheating lovers.

It's the thing Dad said you should never touch, which makes it all the more desirable. The hunt for the key. unlocking the case. The ecstasy of feeling the cool black metal in your hand for the first time—the power contained in the single action which can end with a deafening crack, the acrid odor and lingering evidence on your fingers. The secret sharing with a fellow disobeyer, both relishing the excitement of risking getting caught, not considering the damage to be done. Taking turns playacting like some reckless John Wayne from an old movie. Aiming the gun. One false move, and somebody gets it. The thrill of being so close to doing it.

Lovely, the seductive power of what is forbidden, through the sponsorship of *dangerous situation*. Words like *desirable, ecstasy, secret sharing, relishing the excitement*, and *thrill* bring the family members together and, at least for me, create the excitement I felt as a kid looking at that locked closet.

Lovers cheating are kids playing with a loaded gun.

You thought I wouldn't notice the key on the dresser, the empty box in the nightstand. You and he playing Russian roulette, taking aim at my chest with each whisper, each smile, and touch. My heart beating like a drumroll, building to the point where it might explode with a single shot, spraying any warmth I might have had left all over the both of you. Anger and confusion are fighting for attention as I watch the excitement in your eyes while you play with forbidden toys, feeling satisfied that I could never figure it out, while my eyes fix on you like a laser scope aimed at a deserving target.

Nice use here of the gun family: "Russian roulette," "taking aim at my chest," "explode with a single shot," "forbidden toys," "laser scope aimed at a deserving target."

The linking quality takes Stan on a productive trip in both directions.

SCARLET KEYS

Cheating lover → *dangerous situation* → Target idea: *Smoking crack*

Smoking crack is like having a cheating lover.

One time, what could it hurt? A smoky room, it would soften the moment, the haze would rush around me like warm bath water. I never thought it would be a good thing, I was just curious. Right now, I'm free, living in the thought of it, the thought of it is just a dream, a dream that I can blink away, shake off like rain on my coat. But seeing it, seeing it is a pair of handcuffs, knowledge with no key, a thought tattoo. I open my eyes and breath, I am lost in the flush, I can't believe the rush of what I'm seeing. The smoky grip, the electric hand, squeezing my throat, rushing through my veins like a man punching his fist down each artery. I am breathless and numb as I now know what this is like. It's been here for years waiting, the potential of knowing, then the knowing, like running through fire, the blaze looked so interesting, then the sizzle of skin, the thing I can now not know, the little rocks as they burned and crackled, weaving heat together with no thought of who would see them. They danced, heated and merged and they will leave you like a cl …

Hot spots: "seeing it is a pair of handcuffs," "knowledge with no key," "a thought tattoo," "the blaze looked so interesting, then the sizzle of skin."

Having a cheating lover is like smoking crack.

It's something you say you'll only do once: the rush of driving past his house to see the silhouettes twisting like curling smoke. It's a lighting and adrenaline surging through you when you see it, a set of footprints that turns into a worn path, OCD of the heart, checking the locks, the stove, hiding in bushes, ducking behind trees, checking e-mail, it's a thought that thinks you, the dripping faucet that won't let you sleep, again and again and again, you don't want to see them, but you can't stay away, it's the accident on the freeway, your eyes burn but still, you look, the horror movie, you want to look away but you are rendered motionless, you are no longer yourself, your sanity is a stringed puppet. They are the smoke in your lungs, they are now needles in your heart, there is a thrill in watching them, there is a death that you die every time and yet you can't stop because if you do, it will be done, the smoke will rise and vanish, you will take what you can, touching the bottom of cloud fingers, reaching up to the hem of the ghost of what is still recognizable. It leaves you …

Watch Scarlet stack metaphor on metaphor. Underline them. A compelling picture of the power of suspicion and jealousy.

Your turn. Using *dangerous situation* as your linking quality, find your target idea and take ten minutes to explore it through the lens of *cheating lover.*

Now reverse it and explore *cheating lover* through the lens of your target idea for ten minutes.

DAY #8

FINDING LINKING QUALITIES: WORKING ONE DIRECTION

Prompt: Magnifying Glass

Today you're on your own to find your own linking qualities before you find your target ideas. Today, you'll only move in one direction, exploring your target idea through the lens of *magnifying glass.* After a few days, you'll reverse directions, too.

Now, try this. First, find three interesting qualities (linking qualities) for *magnifying glass.*

Magnifying glass → Linking quality 1:___________

Magnifying glass → Linking quality 2:___________

Magnifying glass → Linking quality 3:___________

Now supply the target idea for each of them.

Magnifying glass → Linking quality 1:________ →
Target idea 1: _________

Magnifying glass → Linking quality 2:_______ →
Target idea 2: __________

Magnifying glass → Linking quality 3:________ →
Target idea 3: _________

Okay, use your first linking quality to find a target idea. Then take ten minutes to explore your target idea through the lens of *magnifying glass.*

STAN SWINIARSKI

Magnifying glass → Linking quality: *Starting a fire by focusing sunlight* → Target idea: *Bully*

A bully is a magnifying glass.

From a distance with the daylight shining on you, you're just like any other dorky kid around here. But I've got a way with light. I can shine it on you, find the one thing about you that you hate so much, that makes you different than the other dweebs. I can focus it with pinpoint accuracy on that singular place on you until I see the smoke, feel the heat rising and watch you squirm, all but bursting into flames with embarrassment. Your tears will be like gasoline, they won't put out the flames. And all the other kids will look on with morbid fascination, because what kid doesn't enjoy a good fire? And maybe a few will even join in on the laughter, proving that I am cooler, more popular, and powerful.

Starting a fire by focusing sunlight is something most people associate with a magnifying glass—an essential quality. It leads Stan to *bully,* and he takes an interesting look at it from the bully's point of view. As usual, a fine group of *magnifying glass*'s family shows up for the fun. The poor kid doesn't have a chance with all that heat.

Now use your own first linking quality to locate a target idea and take ten minutes exploring your target idea through the lens of *magnifying glass.*

YOU: Magnifying glass → Linking quality 1:_______ →
Target idea 1: _______

CAROLINE HARVEY

Magnifying glass → *gets you up close and personal with the object of your desire* →
Target idea: *strip club*

A strip club is a magnifying glass.

The customers hold mugs of beer and lean crooked in their seats at the edge of the small stage, they're glaring at Destiny, the dancer on the 3 a.m. shift. The club, once glittering and clean, is now scuffed at the seams and dingy, the fake black-brown leather of the overstuffed bench seats tearing at their over-worn corners. Too many fat middle-aged asses sitting here and ogling, peering at the dancers with drooling eyes, hungry hearts, desperate bodies. No matter the layered cake of makeup, no matter the sparkle of that sequined bikini, the flash of hundred dollar bills, the clitter clatter of somebody's last quarters thrown onto the floor like a hopeful toss of the dice, no matter the fake names and pocketed wedding rings, the deep truth of it all shows through. The lights flash, the disco ball blushes, nobody can hide here because there's no pretending you're here for something else, nobody goes into a strip club by accident, nobody ends up dancing on a stage in a thong bikini as a mistake—the brutal reality of the moment is all right here, inside the thump thump of raunchy music, in every swirl of hip and shake of tit, in every lean forward and stuff a dollar bill in a bra strap, in every backroom champagne party there is the fact of humanity looming large.

Caroline's work here is interesting: A magnifying glass *magnifies*. Though *magnifying glass*'s family stays in the back room, hidden from view, they allow Caroline to paint the scene in clear and disturbing detail. Without knowing the terms of the metaphor, you'd think it was just a marvelous description, but her linking quality, *gets you up close and personal with the object of your desire,* which took her to the strip club, asks, indeed requires, that she magnify everything. She certainly does.

Now use your second linking quality to find a second target idea. Then take ten minutes exploring your target idea through the lens of *magnifying glass.*

YOU: Magnifying glass → Linking quality 2:______ →
Target idea 2: ________

PAT PATTISON
Magnifying glass → Linking quality 2: *Focuses light to a heated point* →
Target idea 2: *Having an argument.*

Curled in bed, back to back, the air seething, hissing. Sharp tick of the second hand slowing, penetrating the hanging silence, a stabbing. Months of letting it slide, focused to a flashpoint in a few minutes, magnifying, burning like sunlight brought to a point on the back of an ant, cringing, then smoking to an ashed corpse in seconds. All the times you looked away, didn't touch me. All the days I drove home on side roads, delaying, the knot in my belly tightening, hardening the closer I got to home. My footsteps hesitating up the sidewalk—the wineglasses enlarging your eyes.

Okay, use your third linking quality to find another target idea and take ten minutes to explore your target idea through the lens of *magnifying glass.*

YOU: Magnifying glass → Linking quality 3:______ →
Target idea 3: ________

DAY #9

FINDING LINKING QUALITIES: WORKING ONE DIRECTION

Prompt: Swimming Hole

Once again you must find your own linking qualities. Then you'll find your third qualities and, in one direction, explore your target idea through the lens of your first idea *(swimming hole).*

Try this. First, find three interesting qualities (linking qualities) for *swimming hole.*

Swimming hole → Linking quality 1:___________

Swimming hole → Linking quality 2:___________

Swimming hole → Linking quality 3:___________

CHANELLE DAVIS

1. Swimming hole → Linking quality 1: *Entertaining*
2. Swimming hole → Linking quality 2: *Isolated*
3. Swimming hole → Linking quality 3: *You can drown in it*

Using these linking qualities, supply the target idea for each of them. Then take ten minutes to explore your target idea through the lens of *swimming hole.*

1. Swimming hole → Linking quality: *Entertaining* → Target idea: *Busker*

A busker is a swimming hole.

The busker entertained people on the street, underneath a canopy of tall city buildings stretching up towards the summer sun, his music attracting the people until there was a crowd, songs flowing down the street, a river of melody, people diving in and tossing coins, some just lazing around on the park benches, basking, enjoying the day …

Chanelle turns a city street into such a lovely place to hang out, inviting *swimming hole's* family to sit around and hear "songs flowing down the street, a river of melody." Nice job, linking quality! She wouldn't have gotten to busker without you.

2. Swimming hole → Linking quality: *Isolated* → Target idea: *Poet's mind*

A poet's mind is a swimming hole.

The poet's mind is a calm swimming hole, peaceful and deep, he pulls words out and splashes them onto the page in a quiet secluded setting, lines comes to him, rippling along the water like a summer breeze …

Wow, how do you turn a poet's mind into a swimming hole? You link them using *isolated*.

3. Swimming hole → Linking quality: *You can drown in it* → Target idea: *Spring*

Spring is a swimming hole.

Strip off my layers of heavy winter clothing, dive into the pools of daffodils in the park, splashes of pink cherry blossoms and new life flowing through the tree trunks, pouring out the tips of every branch, the weeping willows are ancient green waterfalls, take a big breath of crisp cool air and sparkling smiles …

Sounds a lot like spring at the Victory Gardens in Boston. Look at all the members of *swimming hole's* family spreading their blankets for a lazy afternoon picnic. Chanelle takes an extra metaphorical step to get from drowning to the expressed identity, "dive into the pools of daffodils." Nice.

JESS MEIDER

1, Swimming hole → Linking quality 1: *Refreshing*
2. Swimming hole → Linking quality 2: *Fun*
3. Swimming hole → Linking quality 3: *Cooling*

Using these qualities as linking qualities, supply the target idea for each of them. Then take ten minutes to explore your target idea through the lens of *swimming hole*.

1. Swimming hole → Linking quality: *Refreshing* →
Target idea: *Telling the truth/interacting in love*

Telling the truth/interacting in love is a swimming hole.

Your cool wet words swirl around me like schools of fish, fluttering fast like some low voltage of electricity. I am thrilled by your honesty, it's drinkable, this secret place. At first I sit like a tree, stretching my roots slowly through the soft earth compact and giving way to my gentle push, like fingertips, toe tips, they touch the water that lays languid and deep like your body on my bed, laying there coagulating energies, naked, label-less, pure water, clear, we are transparent, all perception visually shining like puddles in moonlight on the asphalt and sidewalks, glistening emotions that ratify and fortify what we say. Love is the subtle undercurrent that moves around us in a slow whirl, the caress so tepid and freshly aromatic we are swept into its direction, it dances us around, our bodies speckled with diamond splotches of star lights that dangle and float on the surface of this intensely gentle water.

Another victory for our superhero, linking quality, wearing a big scarlet *LQ* on his chest and cape. LO dives in and *refreshes* the relationship, a tough thing to do for a relationship without a waterproof costume.

2. Swimming hole → Linking quality: *Fun* → Target idea: *Square dancing*

Square dancing is a swimming hole.

His lip corners pull back wide across the face as the primal YEEEEEEE slithers thru his teeth at high velocity and dives deep into the HAW and the skip and bounce begin the undulating current of the upright bass woodily humming short quick bomp bomps, limbs stretch wide like swans and then swoop across dancing, kicking legs like a choreographed doggy paddle. Eyes gush with laughter the shine divinely, careening around the room like schools of tiny fish that happily frolic in this space. The caller coaches us into hypnotic patterns that weave and morph in a kaleidoscope, rockets in a swimming pool, the balls of laughter cuckle-ing up and out as heartbeats race in joyous countenance the upheaval of the soul bedazzling the room, an energetic disco ball.

Fun is a pretty abstract linking quality and could take a writer almost anywhere. Jess apparently thinks square dancing is fun and dives in with gusto. The floor is flooded with relatives. Whether you think she's invited too many or not is a matter of personal taste. The point is, third cousins are always in play, whether you want to send them wedding invitations or not. That's the power of the linking qualities.

3. Swimming hole → Linking quality: *Cooling* → Target idea: *Mos Def's song "Creole"*

Mos Def's song "Creole" is a swimming hole.

> His voice is softly cupping the bounty of a gentle water inside, the words are painting a fortune of poems that flutter around me like a warm current, like fingertips underwater smoothly running under and above my skin, energetic waves soften and pond in my heart space. Slow mellow burn of the groove like the hot light of late June, laying its lavish luscious lips all over my face and tangled wet hair curls washed wet then tears pouring out of the strands they retake their original spirals. Words dangle like long limbs from the tall kind thick tree then drop into gentle tensions melodically fall weightless into the pool of his message that continues to sway us back and forth, front against front, swimming in a long kiss in the dark heavy heat of a Beijing August.

What a lovely way to look at a singer's voice. See how important finding a strong linking quality becomes? And you can do it. Easy, right? Okay, do it.

Swimming hole → Linking quality 1:___________
Swimming hole → Linking quality 2:___________
Swimming hole → Linking quality 3:___________

Now, using these qualities as linking qualities, supply the target idea for each of them. Then take ten minutes to explore your target idea through the lens of *swimming hole*.

Swimming hole → Linking quality 1:______ → Target idea 1: ____
Swimming hole → Linking quality 2:______ → Target idea 2: ____
Swimming hole → Linking quality 3:______ → Target idea 3: ___

DAY #10

FINDING LINKING QUALITIES: WORKING ONE DIRECTION

Prompt: Afternoon Nap

Once again you're on your own to find your linking qualities before you find your third qualities. Then move only in one direction, as you explore your target idea through the lens of *afternoon nap*.

Try this. First find three interesting qualities for *afternoon nap.*

Afternoon nap → Linking quality 1:___________

Afternoon nap → Linking quality 2:___________

Afternoon nap → Linking quality 3:___________

Using these qualities as linking qualities, supply the target idea for each of them.

Afternoon nap → Linking quality 1:______ → Target idea 1: ______

Afternoon nap → Linking quality 2:______ → Target idea 2: ______

Afternoon nap → Linking quality 3:______ → Target idea 3: ______

CHANELLE DAVIS

Afternoon nap → Linking quality 1: *Everything slows down*

Afternoon nap → Linking quality 2: *Recharge your body*

Afternoon nap → Linking quality 3: *Close your eyes*

1. Afternoon nap → Linking quality: *Everything slows down* → Target idea: *Autumn*

Autumn is an afternoon nap.

Leaves curl up, slowly sinking into the ground knitting themselves together like a warm blanket, white pillow-shaped clouds hanging in the sky, the earth wrapping itself ready for winter dreaming, soft snoring of crickets outside my window …

Great picture here, with a very effective linking quality. Note how useful simile is in connecting these families. As you saw in day 14 of Challenge #2, simile lets you make a comparison without totally committing to the idea. It keeps you focused on the first term of the comparison rather than sending energy and commitment through to the second term. Much of the family introduction in this challenge has been through the use of simile. Chanelle doesn't commit to a *knitted blanket* with "Leaves curl up, slowly sinking into the ground knitting themselves together like a warm blanket," but she does introduce you to the family member. Simile lets you have it without committing to it. And note her "white pillow-shaped clouds," which aren't real pillows, but hand the pillow a glass of wine to drink outside on the porch, rather than actually coming into the party.

2. Afternoon nap → Linking quality: *Recharge your body* → Target idea: *A holiday*

A holiday is an afternoon nap.

Escape office life, under the palm trees and sunshine, no alarms as hours close their eyes, drifting into each other, dreaming, breathing slowly …

I like how the *hours* close their eyes rather than a person actually taking an afternoon nap on a holiday.

3. Afternoon nap → Linking quality: *Close your eyes* → Target idea: *Kissing*

Kissing is an afternoon nap.

Move my tongue slowly in your mouth, soft dreamy lips relaxing and letting me in, eyes shut tight, feeling your waist with my hands, warm and wrapped in each other like a cocoon …

Only through *close your eyes* can you turn kissing into an afternoon nap. Nice job, linking quality!

SARAH BRINDELL

1. Afternoon nap → Linking quality 1: *Feeling safe*
2. Afternoon nap → Linking quality 2: *Relief from stress*
3. Afternoon nap → Linking quality 3: *Waking up after dark*

1. Afternoon nap → Linking quality 1: Feeling safe → *Mother's smile*

My mother's smile is an afternoon nap.

She glides into the room as sunbeams pour through the open door, soft words breeze the afternoon dust particles around, as they swirl in the golden light toward my pillow. My mother's fluffed gray hair hangs shoulder length in wisps as it tickles my cheek, she whisks it away with her hand and kisses me, accompanied by her famous "muh" sound, gently tugs at the comforter till it tautly binds the bed into a cocoon shape, and there, amidst the luminous beams of floating powder-like dust only visible when daylight hangs low in the sky, her face transforms into an effortless orb of laugh lines surrounded by her hair like a glowing atmosphere. Straining to see it amidst the blinding shafts of sunlight, my eyelids slit, and then close. I am safe and warm in my mother's smile.

A great mom tribute. Linking terms seem almost magical in their power to transform one thing into another, but of course, as you're discovering, there's no magic involved. It's a step-by-step process that almost always yields fresh, interesting discoveries.

2. Afternoon nap → Linking quality 2: *Relief from stress* →
Target idea 2: *Drinking cold soda on a hot day*

Drinking cold soda on a hot day is an afternoon nap.

You feel that first bubbly froth meet your tongue cold and sweet it lulls your thoughts in a lullaby of sips, swallow after swallow, the liquid sputters on a bedlike raft made of lime rinds bound together by sugar, racing toward a misty waterfall that begins at the edge of your throat, catching speed as it drops off past the tonsils, steering through the rapids of your intestinal walls till it settles and collects in crackling pools funneling toward your bladder, assimilating into your sweat glands and bloodstream and as you let go of all worry and drift off into a careless dreamlike sugar buzzzzzzz. The sun melts into the frothy Pacific as the soda melds your muscles into the folding chair, free of the steam and muck that had incessantly risen from the pavement and beaten your throat dry all afternoon. A cold carbonated liquid time-out session that leaves you satiated, finally at peace with the waning heat.

I like "a lullaby of sips." There's a party in your body, and so many of *afternoon nap*'s friends and relatives are invited, courtesy of engraved invitations from *relief from stress*.

3. Afternoon nap → Linking quality: *Waking up after dark* → Target idea: *Realizing that your lover has left you*

Realizing that your lover has left you is an afternoon nap.

He awoke to find all aspects of her gone. The bed was made on her side only, there wasn't even a crease in the sheet where her naked body had been writhing in ecstatic pleasure just a few hours prior. All that light twinkling as it caught the glitter on her cheeks, all those soft words her hips and lips had woven on his chest now unraveled and disintegrated into the night air. The bedroom did have a faint smell of jasmine after dark, when its pungency permeates so heavily that it overwhelms any man within nose-reach, demanding him to indulge in a fantasy for a woman not there, perhaps a one-night-stand woman he could never forget. His bare feet padded across the cold tile floor and toward the door, offering up a few hopeful steps that suggested she might have just slipped into the bathroom for a moment or perhaps was making tea in the kitchen wrapped in that silk wine-stained robe, and soon would return to his side. All rooms revealed nothing but darkness, a hollow dark that somehow enveloped the space and expanded it while he wasn't noticing. Under her spell, he lost himself until there was nothing left of her. He had awakened too late, only aware of her fleeting presence because it didn't exist anymore. The jasmine smell unfurled and escaped out the left-open window, which now emitted a frigid gust of wind as he reached for his evening slippers.

You try.

Afternoon nap → Linking quality 1:___________
Afternoon nap → Linking quality 2:___________
Afternoon nap → Linking quality 3:___________

Using these qualities as linking qualities, supply the target idea for each of them.

Afternoon nap → Linking quality 1:______ → Target idea 1: ______
Afternoon nap → Linking quality 2:______ → Target idea 2: ______
Afternoon nap → Linking quality 3:______ → Target idea 3: ______

DAY #11

FINDING LINKING QUALITIES: WORKING ONE DIRECTION

Prompt: Traffic Cop

Today's exercise is a little different. You will explore your target idea through the lens of *traffic cop*. After finding your linking qualities and doing your usual ten minutes for each one, you'll spend another ten minutes reversing directions, looking at *traffic cop* through the lens of your target idea.

Try this. First find two interesting qualities (linking qualities) for *traffic cop*.

Traffic cop → Linking quality 1: ________________

Traffic cop → Linking quality 2: ________________

Now supply the target idea for each of them.

Traffic cop → Linking quality 1: _______ → Target idea 1: _______

Traffic cop → Linking quality 2: _______ → Target idea 2: _______

CAROLINE HARVEY

Traffic cop → Linking quality: *Stands and points for long periods of time*

Traffic cop → Linking quality: *Stands and points for long periods of time* → Target idea: *A redwood tree*

A redwood tree is a traffic cop.

You are planted there like a monument, unburdened by your forever stillness. Thick roots holding tightly to the ground in strong fists of muscled grip. Underneath you the forest floor shakes awake with crawling insects flicking their stiff legs, furry creatures on the hungry hunt, animals eating and going about the chaotic business of living and dying. You stand stoic and protective, overseeing the orchestration of a city made of dirt and leaf. Your bark is a rippling uniform form-fitted over purposeful flesh, your stance is regal and proud. Your delicate leaves dangle like fingers pointing toward the sun, signaling the direction of freedom; the birds weave themselves around your shape in a choreography of ordered flight. You are the shield that can be counted on to shoulder the brunt of the rain and wind, the armor that does not crumble under pressure, the landmark that indicates how much time has passed between seasons.

Hmmm. What an unusual linking quality. But it really opens up a fresh look at a redwood tree. Caroline even invites *traffic cop*'s cousin, *shield*, into the orchestra. Note also her use of simile, giving the redwood fingers without the necessity of hands. Her use of second person creates a close, personal look at this giant.

Now spend another ten minutes reversing directions, looking at *traffic cop* through the lens of your target idea.

A traffic cop is a redwood tree.

In the middle of the street I stand stoic and sturdy, my feet growing rootlike into the hard crust of road. My legs, strong as trunks and wrapped neatly inside the navy blue bark of my uniform, do not tremble even though the rush of cars feels like a hurricane whipping past me. My arms move in slow purposeful spirals, I exhale into my whistle, the cars crawl by like ants in a line. The sun beats down on the top of my head and under me is a shadow cast in the shape of a brimmed, stiff hat. In my shade a pigeon stops to nibble on a piece of leftover donut. A line of sweat blooms on my brow and the salty moisture drips from my face onto the street. I do not move my still green eyes away from the intersection. I feel as immobile as a dry log.

A lovely turnaround, complete with roots, bark, hurricanes, and ants. Again, an intimate look, and this time she used first-person narrative.

SCARLET KEYS

Traffic cop → Linking quality: *Controlling*

Traffic cop → Linking quality: *Controlling* → Target idea: *A mother*

A mother is a traffic cop.

She stands in the hallway, waving little Johnny out the door, her scream is like a traffic cop's whistle and she blows it for things like forgetting your lunch and leaving with your shoe untied. She hugs her daughter good-bye, she ushers her youngest girl down the stairs and kisses her husband at the door as she waves him good-bye, standing there in the crossfire of other people's lives, shoulders back, strong and steady, arms flailing like a windmill. The family is ordered and their lives keep moving in a steady flow of homework papers, doctor's appointments, napkins forced across stubborn chocolate faces, brooms being pushed, phones answered—the axis that everything and everyone swirls past. She stands there, her beating heart pushing through her housedress against her shiny badge of martyr and master, the badge that is worn down smooth, lackluster and hanging off as she sometimes dreams: the soft lips of a lover on her neck, big soft hands on her hips the feeling of being desired, of being sexy and noticed, a stop sign instead of a speed bump. Or maybe caution, slippery when wet instead of slow, children playing or careful, men working, yield, deer crossing, she wants to strip naked and wave her arms not in warning but in striptease and taunting, remember me, remember who I am, underneath this uniform of formula oatmeal and spit up, there is sweat and passion: This hair should be untied and let lose to fall on my shoul...

Wow! Check out Scarlet's expressed identity "standing there in the crossfire of other people's lives."

Now spend another ten minutes reversing directions, looking at *traffic cop* through the lens of your target idea.

Traffic cop is a mother.

She stands there in the intersection, wearing bright notice-me colors, waving, stopping or waving cars by. Her stomach bulges and pushes over the top of her uniform like play dough squeezed through your hands. She is thick and middle aged, she is tired and stuck, she is the maternal guard of the traffic, whistling orders, checking for seat belts, her voice often unheard, resented, and tolerated. Age spots, sun spots, skin like a leather wallet, feet wide and fat in her black shiny shoes, now her only option is to find purpose in her day of swirling cars and the blare of stereos, the smell of coffee and cigarettes and barking dogs. She's mother to them all, she blows her whistle like she's calling everyone in for dinner, the red and yellow and green light her face and she sweats in the morning sun. Crosswalk, where four lanes meet, what is she left now, they would all come apart ...

In both her pieces, Scarlet uses simile to connect the two literally: "her scream is like a traffic cop's whistle" and "she blows her whistle like she's calling everyone in for dinner." Also note the expressed identity in, "she is the maternal guard of the traffic, whistling orders."

Scarlet's linking quality allows fluid movement between the two keys, *mother* and *traffic cop*. They have a lot in common.

Your turn. Find your two linking qualities and do your usual ten minutes for each one, exploring your target idea through the lens of *traffic cop*. Then spend another ten minutes reversing directions, looking at *traffic cop* through the lens of your target idea.

Traffic cop → Linking quality 1: ________________
Traffic cop → Linking quality 2: ________________

Now supply the target idea for each of them.

Traffic cop → Linking quality 1: ________ → Target idea 1: ______
Traffic cop → Linking quality 2: ________ → Target idea 2: ______

DAY #12

FINDING LINKING QUALITIES: MOVING BOTH DIRECTIONS

Prompt: Wheelchair

Again today, after finding your linking qualities and doing your usual ten minutes exploring your target idea through the lens of *wheelchair,* spend another ten minutes reversing directions, looking at *wheelchair* through the lens of your target idea.

Try this. First find two interesting qualities for *wheelchair.*

Wheelchair → Linking quality 1: ________________
Wheelchair → Linking quality 2: ________________

Now supply the target idea for each of them.

Wheelchair → Linking quality 1: ________ → Target idea 1: _____
Wheelchair → Linking quality 1: ________ → Target idea 2: _____

SUSAN CATTANEO

Linking quality: *It makes you independent*

Wheelchair → Linking quality: *It makes you independent* → Target idea: *Learning how to drive*

Learning how to drive as a wheelchair

Hands frozen like spokes at 10 and 2, your metallic arms stiff with nervousness, the engine whispers, as the tires roll gently forward, seated firmly, your right foot paralyzed on the gas, the dashboard is a blanket over your trembling knees, the traffic flies by with a freedom. You are immobile, your eyes roll right, then left as you venture into the intersection, windshield bracing against the wind to come, your brain brakes at the thought of tailing an 18 wheeler ...

I love "Hands frozen like spokes" and the "dashboard blanket." It takes a while to become independent, but Susan has found an interesting linking quality to join the two families.

Wheelchair as learning how to drive

Feeble, withered string-bean legs, lifted under the thighs and placed in the leather seat, arms hover over the soft black tires, poised to join the highway of wheelchairs zooming up and down the hospital hallway, feet like pedals below, the soft whisper of the tires, the wheeze of brakes, patients roll slowly past rooms, their IVs hanging from metal stands like moving telephone poles, the skip of your heart as you feel the freedom of movement, the open road of life, off ramps waiting to be discovered, confidence revs in your chest, muscles idle in your biceps, then tense as you push forward, you are one with metal and movement ...

What a wonderful moment, "their IVs hanging from metal stands like moving telephone poles." It puts you immediately on the highway. A powerful link.

SCARLET KEYS

Wheelchair → Linking quality: *It makes you independent*

Wheelchair → Linking quality: *It makes you independent* → Target idea: *An adventure novel*

An adventure novel is a wheelchair.

She's never left the United States except for San Diego and South Dakota. Arthritis settled in and she spends more of her life sitting in that soft green chair by the window, book in hand. She doesn't feel bad about never seeing the world, she sees it every day and she pushes up her glasses and sets down her tea. She crosses one short pudgy leg over the other and lets her half socks fall off her feet and picks up her adventure novel. She turns the page and it's like her chair grows wheels and transports her to the world. In one sentence she is eating pasta and melon in a café in Milan. She is looking at Da Vinci's Last Supper, she can feel the warm fingers of an Italian man holding her with moonlight on her face and she holds her breath. You see she says, I've been around the whole world and I've never left this chair, I love the feel of the pages, the smell of the ink, and I never know where I'll end up when I turn another page. I dog-ear the memories I want to read again, I underline the parts that take my breath away and when I'm lonely I read it all again from the beginning, I can do that, I can go back to Milan and feel the 900–year-old stones beneath my tiny sandaled feet and brush the scarf from my neck in the humid July air. I can feel his fingers again and again and stop and read each letter like it's honey dripping from the page. I can kiss him slowly or quickly depending on how fast I read and it's really quite wonderful. Don't feel sorry for me here, sometimes, I wonder if I'm not the lucky one, savoring each moment like I do, stopping at each flower, head down, I know the cracks in the sidewalk, where lovers etch their names and people lose their keys and children drop their ice creams, this is where the life happens, slow down, look down every once in a while, you with the fast-paced life, you with your head in the clouds.

At first I wondered about *adventure novel* as a target idea, but Scarlet goes around the world in it, wheeling like crazy. Note that she accomplishes it through simile, not metaphor, since the relationship between the two ideas is pretty remote. A few second cousins in Milan is about it, but she pulls it off. Thanks, simile!

A wheelchair is an adventure novel.

This chair is all she's ever known, she's never walked, this is her life on wheels, her mobile home and she hands out smiles like pennies in your beggar's cup and she shames you with her gratitude and glides down the sunny side of the street. Every day is adventure, every street is like the turning of a page, her wheelchair is her adventure novel and she can't wait to find out how it's all going to turn out. She watches life unfold before her, flowers bloom and burst like she's inside a painting watching the master's next stroke of the brush. She glides along in constant

> wonder at why the birds sing, what are they saying, the smell of the hotdogs and the french fries in the park. She reaches out for every dog she passes and laughs at the soft Bichon Frise and the wiry terrier's fur. It's always been magic for her, what's going to happen next? Leaves pattern the ground, clouds take shape and she stops to see the castle and then she closes her eyes and the sunshine is a mystic dragon and she's up in her ivory tower, then she hears a guitar playing and she's in Portugal the sun is setting and she wiggles her toes in the warm south sun. She can bookmark her days and has so many wonderful memories, she picked them all, she has a passport to the stars and that steel cloth covered back is like the spin of a book.

This turnaround works beautifully. It paints such a positive and inspiring picture. Like all great metaphor, it changes the way you see things. I'll see this every time I see a wheelchair. Thanks, Scarlet. Thanks, linking quality.

Your turn. Find your two linking qualities and do your usual ten minutes for each one, exploring your target idea through the lens of *wheelchair.* Then spend another ten minutes reversing directions, looking at *wheelchair* through the lens of your target idea.

Wheelchair → Linking quality 1: ________________
Wheelchair → Linking quality 2: ________________

Now supply the target idea for each of them.

Wheelchair → Linking quality 1: _______ → Target idea 1: ______
Wheelchair → Linking quality 1: _______ → Target idea 2: ______

DAY #13

FINDING LINKING QUALITIES: MOVING BOTH DIRECTIONS

Prompt: Sailboat

Once again, after finding your linking qualities and taking the usual ten minutes to explore your target idea through the lens of *sailboat,* you'll spend another ten minutes reversing directions, looking at *sailboat* through the lens of your target idea.

Try this. First find two interesting qualities for *sailboat*.

Sailboat → Linking quality 1: ________________

Sailboat → Linking quality 2: ________________

Using these qualities as linking qualities, supply the target idea for each of them.

Sailboat → Linking quality 1: _______ → Target idea 1: ________

Sailboat → Linking quality 2: _______ → Target idea 2: ________

CHANELLE DAVIS

Linking quality 1: *Moves with wind*

Sailboat → Linking quality: *Moves with wind* → Target idea: *Leaves*

Leaves are sailboats.

Yellow leaves, all lined up along the branch, like boats docked at a jetty, rocking side to side, one by one they cast off into the cool air, sails stretched out, catching gusts of wind and gliding over the ocean of grass, like explorers searching for somewhere to land on their maiden voyage …

Again, simile charges in and lines the leaves up along the branch. Though Chanelle shows the reader *boats,* the focus stays on the *leaves*. That's because *like* is such a great energy blocker—it blocks the energy from transferring to the second term, *boats*. There's a huge difference between the simile, "Yellow leaves, all lined up along the branch, *like* boats docked at a jetty," and "Yellow leaves, all lined up along the branch, *are* boats docked at a jetty," which transfers *leaves'* energy to *boats*. The rest of the piece invites some of *sailboat*'s more gorgeous family members to the party.

Sailboats are leaves.

A sailboat crumples on the rocks, drifting down into the coral playground, shiny new yellow paint slowly rotting below the waves …

Crumples. Yup!

JESS MEIDER

Linking quality: *Graceful*

Sailboat → Linking quality: *Graceful* → Target idea: *Beautiful woman in heels*

A beautiful woman in heels is a sailboat.

She's a beauty, natural, handcrafted, the pink-beige satin silk like sails that stretch long and up from her delicate ankles to her wide open collarbone, the skin dipping in like a sensual cavern just above it. A simple gem catches the afternoon sun, bringing the eye to feast up on the smooth skin taut to catch the energy blowing in, the deep orange glow of the sun's repeal only enhances her bowing shape, how the silk wraps around hips that offer the soft rounded flesh of her belly, each rib curved and formed to meet her chest, creases of the silk flowing like grains of a smooth wood that has been steamed and heated and shaped to fit her like a perfect glove. She glides, not one bump to reveal her steps; no, her figure sways slowly, to the left, mmm, to the right, her head gliding along a horizon, floating thru the crowds like a soft smiling wind, eyes dazzled; she gathers it up and fuels her glide, as graceful as a southern gentle wind that seagulls surf and soar upon.

Hot spots: "creases of the silk flowing like grains of a smooth wood," "She glides, not one bump to reveal her steps; no, her figure sways slowly, to the left, mmm, to the right, her head gliding along a horizon," and "as graceful as a southern gentle wind."

A sailboat is a beautiful woman in heels.

Antoine plays about the medium-sized boat like an intuitive lover, touching her, pulling softly, her sails gently lift to catch a fine sea breeze, he smoothes his hand along her graceful curves, and only takes his hands on to her wheel when absolutely necessary. She is carrying us in her graceful glide along the aqua blues and greens, lifting us away from the white Greek homes that look more and more like dots on a cliff's painting. I am most impressed and mesmerized by Antoine's careful encouraging touch. He is in control, but in the right way: a dancing motif, his body leading her body, they are languid, loving, sexy, impetuous, teasing, a sailing foreplay of wind water wood that glides like a feminine goddess figure across the crowds, on towards the sun setting light show ahead of us in the west.

Both the sailboat and the woman glide beautifully, in "a sailing foreplay of wind water wood that glides like a feminine goddess figure across the crowds." A convergence of tanned, beautiful families, brought to you through the sponsorship of *graceful*, and tacking elegantly in both directions.

Your turn. Again, find your two linking qualities and spend the usual ten minutes on each one, exploring your target idea through the lens of *sailboat*. Then, spend another ten minutes reversing directions, looking at *sailboat* through the lens of your target idea.

Sailboat → Linking quality 1: ________________

Sailboat → Linking quality 2: ________________

Using these qualities as linking qualities, supply the target idea for each of them.

Sailboat → Linking quality 1: ______ → Target idea 1: _________

Sailboat → Linking quality 2: ______ → Target idea 2: _________

DAY #14

FINDING LINKING QUALITIES: MOVING BOTH DIRECTIONS

Prompt: Vacation

Congratulations! You've made it to day 14. For the last day of the challenge, after finding your linking qualities and exploring your target idea through the lens of *vacation* for the usual ten minutes, you'll spend another ten minutes reversing the direction, looking at *vacation* through the lens of your target idea.

Try this. First find two interesting qualities for *vacation*.

Vacation → Linking quality 1: ________________

Vacation → Linking quality 2: ________________

Using these qualities as linking qualities, supply the target idea for each of them.

Vacation → Linking quality 1: ______ → Target idea 1: ________
Vacation → Linking quality 2: ______ → Target idea 2: ________

CLARE MCLEOD

Linking quality: *Long overdue*

Vacation → Linking quality: *Long overdue* → Target idea: *Library book*

A library book is a vacation.

Each word is a grain of sand and I'm sinking into them like a tide is pulling me into the water. Absorbed into a new world, there's no way I'll skip ahead to the ending, I want it to last. I follow the horizon of lines that lay before me on the page, unconsciously holding my breath as particular passages chop and twist. Sometimes gliding along the stories' highway, speeding through frictionless territory until some detour appears, then lost in the unfamiliar. I only have a short time though til I return ...

These two ideas work so well together, but the key to getting there is the linking quality, *long overdue*. Then there's the realization, "Yes, a book can take you somewhere you've never been before."

A vacation is a library book.

I borrow the town of Lucca for a while, someplace thousands have seen before, all kinds, leaving the oils of their skin behind. It is bound by walls, fortified. The smell of leather hangs overripe and the buildings are yellowed and peeling. After a day wandering its streets, my tired eyes droop and I can go no further. The ...

I was really curious to see how this could turn around and was startled to see a whole town invite *library book*'s family right into the middle of the square with *borrow, bound, smell of leather, yellowed and peeling,* and *tired eyes droop.* Clare makes me want to become an avid reader of exotic places.

SARAH MOUNT

Linking quality: *Calming*

Vacation → Linking quality: *Calming* → Target idea: *Being held by a lover*

Being held by a lover is a vacation.

Being held in the warm tide of my lover's arms, standing firm as my feet sink slowly into the disappearing ground. I close my eyes as his cheeks kiss me—a cool wind, silencing the background. He speaks sunshine words into my neck, his blue-sky eyes keeping me right here, now, this is the only important thing. The heavy beating of my heart muffled by his whisper "breathe with me". Our chests rising …

A wonderful intermingling of relatives here. Underline all of Sarah's *vacation* words and note how friendly they are to her lover. A match made under blue-sky eyes.

A vacation as being held by a lover

The weight of the week finally comes to a close. I see the clouds separate and rays of sunlight enclose me like a lover's arms. I sip my drink cool as a sweet French kiss, letting my feet be swallowed by soft sand. Closing my eyes to the whisper of waves, a warm breath of wind sends shudders up my spine. I retreat into the sea, stepping all the way in, the salt kissing every inch of my skin—foamy fingerprints I'll wear like a medal. The water over my head, I breathe with the tide, no footprints to leave behind.

The simile "rays of sunlight enclose me like a lover's arms" comes racing in to set up the turnaround, followed by the *as* form of the simile, "my drink cool as a sweet French kiss." Yum.

I love "foamy fingerprints I'll wear like a medal." Nicely done.

Your turn. Again, find your two linking qualities and do your usual ten minutes for each one, exploring your target idea through the lens of *vacation*. Then spend another ten minutes reversing directions, looking at *vacation* through the lens of your target idea.

Vacation → Linking quality 1: _______________

Vacation → Linking quality 2: ________________

Using these qualities as linking qualities, supply the target idea for each of them.

Vacation → Linking quality 1: ________ → Target idea 1: _______
Vacation → Linking quality 2: ________ → Target idea 2: _______

Yippie! That's it!

Now take a little time off and let your bloodstream absorb this process of looking at ideas. But do come back soon. A final challenge awaits (or looms), and it'll (fill in a metaphor here) you in unexpected ways.

CHALLENGE #4

WRITING IN RHYTHM & RHYME

True Ease in Writing comes from Art, not Chance,
As those move easiest who have learn'd to dance.

—ALEXANDER POPE, "AN ESSAY ON CRITICISM"

I got the idea for this challenge from Gillian Welch, who several years ago participated in an object-writing group with me and four others. We worked online every Tuesday for several months and then, because we were having such a great time, we decided to add a second night. So every Tuesday and Thursday, I dutifully sent out the "object for the day," and, using "reply all," we each sent our efforts to the others. I highly recommend group writing like this, if you can find several good writers to join in.

Gillian's partner David Rawlings had suggested to her that there be a tighter link between object writing and actual lyric writing, and Gillian responded by suggesting to the group that we try writing in *tetrameter* (four stressed syllables per line) *couplets* (rhyming in groups of two) every other Thursday. "I've been doing it recently," she said. "You don't get as much written, but it's pretty interesting, and I've been able to export some of it directly into my songs."

We tried it, and both the results and the changes in approach were fascinating.

In the following challenge, you'll work for several days in tetrameter couplets, in both triple and duple meter. Then you'll switch to common meter, after which you'll work in two larger forms, employing some pentameter lines. It'll take a little preparation, though. You'll have to spend some time looking at rhythm and rhyme.

First, let's talk about rhythm.

RHYTHM: STRESSED SYLLABLES

You create rhythm in language by arranging stressed and unstressed syllables into patterns.

Right. I guess if you're going to arrange stressed and unstressed syllables into patterns, it would be very helpful to be able to tell stressed and unstressed syllables apart. So start with that.

When you hear someone speaking a language that you don't understand, they seem to talk very fast. All you hear is an uninterrupted stream of syllables, and you have no way to distinguish where words start or end. As far as you can hear, each syllable might be a separate word, or maybe there are words made up of several syllables. If you don't know the language, you won't be able to tell.

The purpose of language is to communicate ideas as efficiently as possible. To that end, people talk pretty fast, or at least, they don't pause between the words in our sentences. They speak *legato*—smoothly without stopping. That's why words come in a steady stream and seem to go by so fast when you don't understand them. Languages all have strategies to allow speakers to be efficient (speak legato) and yet know which syllables can stand alone and which ones clump together to form a single word. In English, you use pitches to create melodic shapes. Pitches give English speakers a second way (besides sound) to identify multisyllabic words. For example, the word *release* has two syllables. When you learn the word, you learn not only the sounds of the syllables, but also a little melody and rhythm. In effect, you learn to sing it. Like this:

re**lease** da DUM

The second syllable is higher in pitch. Say it several times, then slow it down and listen to the pitches. You should hear a melodic leap of a fourth on "lease"—(do fa). That way you can say something like "The release mechanism is opposite the receiver" without pausing, and everyone will understand "release" to be two syllables joined together to denote one idea. And it doesn't even sound like you're talking fast, since the melodies identify the multisyllabic words. You only "hear" four ideas: release, mechanism, opposite, receiver.

Learn to hear the shape of the language—to pay attention to pitches as well as sounds. That way, when a word has several syllables, its pitches help identify it as one word even though it is embedded in a steady stream of syllables.

Every word with two or more syllables has a melodic shape: One or more syllables have higher pitches than the others. They are called *stressed syllables*. Stressed syllables are usually a major fourth (fa) above the "tonic" (do) established by the unstressed syllables.

Look at these:

unkind butcher unconscious opposite consequences interrupted

Say each one a few times normally, then pay attention to the pitches.

un**kínd** (do fa) **butch**er (fa do)

Un**cón**scious (do fa do) has three syllables; only one of them stressed.

Óppo**síte** also has three syllables, but two are stressed, the first being stronger than the last. It is called the *primary stress*. When there are two or more stressed syllables in a word, one is highest in pitch and is usually a step above the *secondary stress*—(sol do fa). In this case, the primary stress is the first syllable of **opposite**. Multisyllabic words with more than one stressed syllable will contain a secondary stress.

Cónse**quén**ces has four syllables, two of them stressed. The primary stress is on "con," which has the highest pitch (sol) when we say the word. The *secondary stress* "quence" is also stressed (fa), just not as much. You should hear (sol do fa do).

Ínter**rúp**ted has four syllables, two of them stressed. Which one is the primary stress? Yup, the third syllable (fa do sol do).

To determine stressed syllables in a multisyllabic word, just listen to the pitches. They'll let you know every time. Multisyllabic words are pretty easy; you can be sure of this because people agree on them. At least their primary stress is listed in our book of agreements—the dictionary.

But how about one-syllable words, the staple of English and especially of lyrics? Don't bother looking in the dictionary; it doesn't mark stresses on one-syllable words.

One-syllable words are stressed when they have an important job to do, like delivering a message. Nouns, verbs, adjectives, and adverbs all get sweaty because they work hard, like these:

track list risk luck slick hard stem strip

Because their function is to carry meaning (a cognitive function), they will *always* be stressed. Humans learn as children to raise the pitch of their voices when pronouncing these words to show that they are important. These raised pitches act as spotlights that shine on these words and draw attention to them. Again, they will usually be raised somewhere between a third and fifth above the tonic (do) set by the unstressed syllable.

Other one-syllable words have a different function—a grammatical function. Think of them as sign carriers. Their job is to show how the important words relate to each other. They also set the tonic (do) that allows the raised pitches to shine. Look at:

The **days** of **wine** and **ro**ses

It is easy to pick out the stressed syllables, but look at the others:

- *The* is an article. Its job is to tell us there is a noun coming.

- *Of* is a preposition showing that the days contain the wine and roses.
- *And* is a conjunction showing us that wine belongs with roses; they are in the same boat. They are both possessed by the days.

These sign carriers are humble. They stay out of the limelight, content with their lower pitches, and help organize things by establishing the fundamental tone. Without them, sentences would be in chaos. Here is a list of some of these workers. In most cases, they will be unstressed.

prepositions (e.g., of, to, after, over)
articles (e.g., a, the)
conjunctions (e.g., and, or, but)
auxiliary verbs indicating tense (e.g., have run, had run)
auxiliary verbs indicating mood (e.g., might run, may run)
personal pronouns (e.g., I, him, their)
relative pronouns (e.g., which, who, when)

Of course, any of these can be stressed when a contrast is involved.

I asked you to throw the ball **tó** me, not **át** me.
I asked you to throw the ball to **mé**, not to **hér**.
I asked **yóu** to throw the ball, not **hím**.

You'll be able to tell. Just use your ears and your common sense.

Compound Words

There are some two-syllable words that contain both a primary and secondary stress. These are unusual, but easily recognized, since they are usually made up of two separate words that would be stressed if they appeared alone, called *compound words*. Like these:

hotdog sunlight nighttime newsstand pigtail sandstorm

In English, the primary stress in compound words is almost always on the first syllable.

Secondary Stress in Grammatical Functions

Articles, prepositions, and conjunctions, because their job is to show relationships between meaning functions, are usually unstressed. They have a grammatical (or secondary) function. Yet many prepositions have two or more syllables and thus contain, within themselves, more and less stressed syllables. For example, *óver* has a stronger first syllable, while the second syllable is stronger in *befóre*. Generally these stronger syllables rise a major third (mi) above the tonic set by the unstressed syllable.

Because prepositions are not as important as the nouns, verbs, adjectives, and adverbs they serve, their stressed syllables are marked with a secondary stress (//), which also notes their secondary function in the line. Because of this, when you set lyric to melody, you will remember to relegate prepositions to secondary rhythmic positions in the bar.

Take a second to notice *into*, another two-syllable preposition. It is stressed **ín**to, not in**tó**. It is probably the most badly handled word in songwriting—perhaps since it usually follows a stressed syllable:

> She walked into the room.

The proper handling is

> She walked (pause) **ín**to the room.

not

> She walked in**to** the room.

'Nuff said.

Rhythm

Again, you create rhythm in language by arranging stressed and unstressed syllables into patterns. The most usual pattern, typical of 4/4 time, is a duple (two) pattern:

> da DUM, or DUM da

When you repeat the pattern a few times, you produce a duple rhythm:

da DUM da DUM da DUM da DUM
I **soon** for**got** the **ones** I **loved**

Or

DUM da DUM da DUM da DUM da
Don't let **lov**ers **leave** you **strand**ed

Since the pattern was repeated four times, there are four stressed syllables in the line and thus a **tetra**meter line in duple meter.

Lyrics and poetry also work with triple rhythms, typical of 3/4, 6/8, and 12/8 time signatures:

da da DUM da da DUM da da DUM da da DUM
In the **still** of the **night** when I **held** you so **tight**

Or

DUM da da DUM da da DUM da da DUM da
Roses have **thorns** that can **cut** you to **pie**ces

Again, since the pattern was repeated four times, there are four stressed syllables in the line and thus a **tetra (four)** meter line in triple meter.

Of course, lines need not be regular, and in fact, in this challenge it is better that your lines be a little jagged. Writing in four-stress lines is limiting enough. Writing in regular four-stress lines would let the rhythm drive the bus. A line like this (by Paul Simon):

Four in the morning, crapped out, yawning

Is a tetrameter line:

Four in the **morning**, **crapped** out, **yawn**ing

But it is hardly regular, containing a triple pattern (DUM da da) and three duple patterns (DUM da). For a time, you'll be working in four-stress lines, the mainstay for songwriters (along with trimeter lines), because they suit the demands of 4/4 time so perfectly.

Or this (by Sting):

I can **hot**wire an ig**nit**ion like **some** kind of **star**

So you can be somewhat relaxed in constructing your lines. Just make sure they have only four stresses.

For the first two days, you'll work in rhythm without rhyme, after which you'll jump into couplets, before moving on to other line lengths and rhyme schemes.

Have a good fourteen days.

DAY #1

TETRAMETER LINES

This begins the last of the four challenges, and it is intended to use all the skills you've gained so far. Keep your writing sense-bound, and keep your eyes open for metaphor.

As usual, set a timer and respond to the following prompts for exactly the time allotted. Use only tetrameter lines, concentrating on a duple feel. No rhymes for now.

Sight **Sound** **Taste** **Touch** **Smell** **Body** **Motion**

10 minutes: Sunset

CHANELLE DAVIS

Peeling rays of orange light
Juices dripping through the clouds
Flung across the rippling ocean
Swirling blue to black in minutes
The moon rushes the sun away
Hungry for the stage and a crowded street

Cool night air chills me
Slipping its fingers under my scarf

CLARE MCLEOD

Sinking into the horizon's trees
The sun's burnt amber disc
Is swallowed whole by the green tongues
I pull the scarf around me tighter
As a light breeze picks up my hair
The twilight air is a little chill
And the purple time descends gentle
Turning, I head for warmth and home

Look at their use of metaphor. Pretty cool, "night air ... slipping its fingers under my scarf," and the forest as "green tongues" swallowing the sun. Count the stressed syllables for practice. Then it's your turn.

5 minutes: Art Museum

TAMI NEILSON

Walls a crisp and sterile white
Like bed sheets on a hospice ward
No sound but heels that click and scuff
Echo, bounce off concrete floors
Colour pops to life in frames
I almost smell the paint not dried
While brushes whisper canvas secrets

SCARLET KEYS

Swirling twirling dance hall dress
Kicking legs, white petticoats
Porcelain bosom cancan dance
Beer mustaches sway and ask
To let me turn to liquid now
Slipping off this canvas now

To feel her tiny hand in mine
Across this crowded museum floor

Really nice use of senses here. The "I almost smell the paint not dried" and "feel her tiny hand in mine." Both pieces pull you in. Go ahead, pull me in. It's your turn.

DAY #2

TETRAMETER LINES

Now that you have a feel, from yesterday, for tetrameter lines, do it again, to lock it in. As usual, keep your writing sense-bound and your eyes open for metaphor.

Set your timer and respond to the following prompts for exactly the time allotted. Use only tetrameter lines, concentrating on creating a duple feel (moving in twos).

Mary had a little lamb is a duple feel.
Mary, she had the littlest lamb is a triple feel.

No rhymes till tomorrow.

Sight Sound Taste Touch Smell Body Motion

10 minutes: Digging for Gold

SUSAN CATTANEO

Sand and silt and painted earth
Kneeling down in rushing water
Feel the frosty bite of cold
Pan in hand, sifting, shaking
Golden sparks shine in sun
Matted moustache spitting chaw
Squinty eyes and cavern chest
Leather boots sucking mud
A circling hawk spins in flight

Kicking up the desert dust
Hand trembling, heavy metal
Gleaming, yearning, jealous rage
Pulling hearts, boasting, brawling
Heavy fists swing and sway
Muscles tense and whiskey slow
Fill your mouth with blood and dirt

SARAH BRINDELL

Your fingernails collect the dirt
as each hand pushes further
hoping that with every grab
you'll find, inside the brown, some yellow
so bright, the sun surrenders
Who cares if this apartment yard's
been excavated long before
and many kids have searched in vain?
Maybe they all missed a spot …
As dinner permeates the air
You know your time is running short
Just then a glimmer grabs your eye …

Both of these examples use the duple rhythm well. Note that the lines with feminine endings (water, shaking, metal, brawling, further, yellow, surrenders) still retain the duple rhythms.

Your turn.

5 minutes: Pickup Truck

PAT PATTISON

Smell the tires that stripe the asphalt
Smoke and rust and burning oil
Wrists and forearms show the veins
Grip the wheel and fill your bed
Cool black earth in barrow's heaps
Or gravel shorn from solid rock

Groan beneath the heavy load
Truck that bends it back for you
Sweaty slave in iron chains
Pull the slabs to pyramids

CHANELLE DAVIS

Limping down the empty highway
Wrinkled paint in shades of blue
Coughing motor stops and starts
Headlights squinting through the night

Working in second person can be effective. It allows you to write actively, sometimes using commands instead of statements. And look at the personification in "Truck that bends it back for you" and "Headlights squinting through the night."

Your turn.

DAY #3

TETRAMETER COUPLETS

A tetrameter couplet is a pair of tetrameter lines that rhyme. Like these:

There's a wire in my jacket. This is my trade
It only takes a moment, don't be afraid

Whose woods these are I think I know
His house is in the village though

Today you'll add rhyme to the mix. Keep your writing sense-bound, and keep your eyes open for metaphor. If you need help with rhyme, please check out pages 37-43 in *Writing Better Lyrics* and take special note of the effects of rhyme types. For a more complete handling, see my *Essential Guide to Rhyming.*

Here's a sample from the online writing group:

Avalanche (10 minutes)

GILLIAN WELCH

It'll bury you and carry you and pin you to the bottom
You will suffocate in minutes boys so smoke 'em if you got 'em
And the weight on your chest is as nothing to the sound
Of the blood in your ears and the mountain crashing down
Oh the avalanche has got you and it will not let you go
You are sucked up in the slipstream of fusilage and snow
You are dancing with the witches in the Mardi Gras parade
Arms akimbo as you limbo in a bloody bone glissade
Oh the avalanche has got you and will secret you away
To the sea beyond the sun where there is no night or day
Where the grass is never green and the peaches never fall
And tomorrow there will be no dawn at all
But the limousines were wrong and the coffins weren't right
Death is white death is white death is white

PAT PATTISON

Tumbling and tumbling, boulders and rocks
Fallen away from the red mountain top
Dust on the horses, dust on the town
Dust like a ghost cloud swirls all around
Color of blood, the color of pain
Some of these children won't breathe it again
Crack of the mountain narrow and torn
Safe from the bite of the big winter storms
The risk that you take to be safe from the wind
The risk that you take to be close to your friends
The voice of the mountain still ringing so clear
Thunder at sunrise, the chill rush of fear
Stones hurtle downward, growling and wild
Send them to rest in the valley a while

SUSAN CATTANEO

Roaring down the emerald chutes

Trees on either side salute
The cackle of wind and the cart wheeling rocks
The snow takes the hits, the bumps and the shocks
Screeching with glee, picking up speed
Pigtails of snow, frosty white cheeks
Crumble and rest at the base of the hill
Icicle lungs breathing still

SHANE ADAMS

She broke my heart with a white-scented letter
The "we'll be friends" tag didn't make me feel better
A postscript as soft as her angora sweaters
And all of the cunning of Las Vegas bettors
Intrusive and cold as a credit card creditor
I bleed in the jaws of a relationship predator
Regretting the day that I ever bedded her
I knew long ago that I should've just shedded her
But even back then I knew we had no chance
So I suffocate in this white, three-hole punched, college-ruled paper avalanche

SCARLET KEYS

The cookies were crumbling and tumbling fast
His teeth bit right through them like cold breaking glass
The avalanche sputtered with each bite he took
Pieces of cookies peppered his book
Caught in the story right through the big quake
Chocolate and sugar covered the page
Little desperate crumbs in the side of his mouth
Like a dozen spring skiers holding their ground
Clinging for safety like small chocolate chips
In the mustache like tree limbs losing their grip

As usual, set a timer and respond to the following prompts for exactly the time allotted. Use only tetrameter lines, creating couplets by **rhyming lines in pairs**. And this time, feel free to vary your rhythms with both duple and triple feel. Remember,

Mary had a little lamb is a duple feel.
Mary, she had the littlest lamb is a triple feel.

But stay with four stresses per line.

Sight **Sound** **Taste** **Touch** **Smell** **Body** **Motion**

10 minutes: Mountain

GILLIAN WELCH

I remember as a child I was looking at the mountain
At the penny bright leaves and the river dark fountain
And the brushy willow bending and the granite all a-shiver
And the quiet pine a-standing by the sudden laughing river
And I looked at the sky and I looked at the ground
And I wondered at the mountain that could bring the night down
In a silent creeping shadow like a vapor like a stain
Spreading out and deepening and emptying the vein
Spilling down into the valley from the lee side to the plain
And there it cast a shadow like a place with out a bottom
There was summer in the meadow but on the mountain it was autumn
Made a worry in your bones just to pass beneath the pall
With a lonesome kind of empty like a cupboard on the wall
And a withered kind of purple like the fruit upon the ground
That's the color of the mountain that could bring the night down

KEPPIE COUTTS

Rising up like a bicep curl
Ridges and rims unfold and unfurl
The earth like the face of an ancient man
Twisting his smile and making the land
Houses sprout in Los Angeles
In places you never think they would be
Nestled into the crust and folds
Of the mountains that frame the glittering gold
The Hollywood sign is an acne scar

From a teenage romance that went too far
The boulevard is a magazine
With pages torn out and glutting the streets
The mountains behind must sigh as they watch
The pimples swell until they pop

The metaphors and similes are wonderful. Go ahead and underline them. Can you feel the triple meter in both? The rhymes are mixtures of perfect and other assorted rhyme types. Remember when you're doing yours that the whole rhyming panoply is available. Use them, especially when you're on the hunt for a rhyme match.

Now, try it.

5 minutes: Snowstorm

CHANELLE DAVIS

I hear her rattling the kitchen door
Whipping the roof and chilling the floor
Her breath is angry and restless tonight
Screaming through the huddled pines
The streets are devoured in clouds of snow
And the stars shiver with nowhere to go

BLEU

Blurry and furious blusterous wind
Stinging your face like millions of pins
You can't feel your fingers or find your direction
The road disappeared in a coat of confection
This stuff is so frigid you can't call it snow
It's more like the sky is just dropping small stones
You trudge through the white at significant angle
And pray that the storm is too weak to strangle
You struggle and stumble and crash to your knees
And feel your throat squeeze as your vocal chords freeze

Again, the metaphors are lovely. Also note the personification in Chanelle's and the use of second person in Bleu's. Some nice rhyming with tonight/pines, wind/pins, snow/stones. Notice especially how they "open" the couplets and make them move. That's what creates instability, which can be very expressive in itself, like a film score enhancing the meanings of the words.

Your turn.

DAY #4

TETRAMETER COUPLETS

Keep your writing sense-bound, and keep your eyes open for metaphor. As usual, set a timer and respond to the following prompts for exactly the time allotted. Use only tetrameter lines, creating couplets by rhyming lines in pairs. Feel free to vary your rhythms with both duple and triple feel.

Sight Sound Taste Touch Smell Body Motion

10 minutes: Train

GILLIAN WELCH

Slowly with a puffing and a pulling and a chugging
It is moving like a mountain with a hundred horses tugging
Now just a little faster you can see the wheels a-turning
You can hear the steam a-hissing you can smell the diesel burning
In the silent sliding window see the wishers who are waving
Into daylight as we jettison the platform and the paving
Then the scrappy city fences and the blur of the trees
And then the old conductor will be taking tickets please

BLEU

Like African drums way off in jungle
Calling to you with a rippling rumble
You slip out the window and into the black

Feeling your way to the rusty old track
A faint star appears too close to the ground
And you know that it's coming, no stopping it now
Then comes the whistle, changing in pitch
From lower to higher, your heart starts to twitch
And now you can feel the wood shaking in time
And smell the coal burning, and see the smoke rise
As the iron rushes forward you raise up your fists
And scream at the engine and the world in the mist
You stare down that killer, and don't move an inch
'Til it's one breath away, and you're laughing in the ditch

Note Gillian's use of all feminine rhymes, until the last couplet, which ends nicely with the one-syllable masculine rhyme trees/please. They are all perfect rhymes. Look at Bleu's rhymes and try to name the different rhyme types. Both use triple rhythms well, making the train really move.

Your turn.

5 minutes: Sleeping Late

KEPPIE COUTTS

Like fireflies in a frenzy of light
Flickers of dreams still dance in my mind
A frolic of faces that whisper my name
And tempt me with secrets if I promise to stay
But morning arrives in a pulsing of waves
Swimming and sliding and half awake
Finally breaching the shallow surface
Sunlight streaming through open curtains

BLEU

The sound bangs your head like a hammer to gong
A series of sounds more like screams than a song
You squeeze your eyes, they're pretending they're dead
But you make out some numbers blinking bright red

11:11 never looked so damn evil
And the torture you're feeling seems almost medieval
Your breath hits your nose and you smell last night's booze
As you fall out of bed straight into your shoes

Both Keppie and Bleu use *identity* rather than rhyme in: waves/awake and evil/medieval. Note how the sounds don't feel like they connect—that's typical of identities. Lovely metaphors and similes in both.

Your turn.

DAY #5

TETRAMETER COUPLETS

Keep your writing sense-bound, and keep your eyes open for metaphor. As usual, set a timer and respond to the following prompts for exactly the time allotted. Use only tetrameter lines, creating couplets by rhyming lines in pairs. Feel free to vary your rhythms with both duple and triple feel.

Sight **Sound** **Taste** **Touch** **Smell** **Body** **Motion**

10 minutes: John Brown

GILLIAN WELCH

Who is that raging cauldron that is hissing where he's sitting
That is fuming like a geyser and sulphuriously spitting
Now he's leaping to his feet with his fists in the air
And his eyes are slowly burning through a cumulous of hair
Wilder than a wolverine starting to unravel
He is brandishing and hollering and pounding like a gavel
And shouting like a madman with the fire coming down
But this is not a madman this is John Brown
A Baptist in a buckskin with the spirit in his bones
That has taken him and shaken him and claimed him as its own

Possessed him like the demons that go raving through the night
It has lead him to the bottom of the world without a light
What is this fatal whip that will not let him be
Just a whisper in his head that said every man is free
It will take him in the end sure as morning sure as hunger
It will wrap him round the deepest roots and slowly drive him under
But the words will remain when he goes in the ground
This man died for freedom this is John Brown

PAT PATTISON

John Brown John Brown
Come and lay your body down
Smell the coffin, smell the ground
Hear the bootsteps comin' round
Pitchforks raised against the night
Wrapped in sheets, clean and white
Color's gonna bring you down
John Brown John Brown

Both of these are basically tetrameter lines. Though my first line has only four syllables, each one is stressed, creating an almost marching feel, as opposed to the expansive line "Possessed him like the demons that go raving through the night." Note the nice mix of masculine and feminine rhymes in Gillian's, combined with wonderful metaphors and similes.

Your turn.

5 minutes: Broken Glass

JESS MEIDER

Pierce the callous thick skin
Wishes shatter, punctured like pins
Zing! the stab flashes into the brain
A sharp shard of hope revisits me again
Glassified tears that hit the floor with a crash
They tinkle one by one smash, crack

PAT PATTISON

Scattered diamonds dust the path
Grab the sunlight, shoot it back
Shattered wineglass tossed away
Eyes narrowed, crimson face
Screaming lungs and curling fists
Duck and cover, fuse is lit
Blue to black to yellow stain
Turn your stomach, sweat like rain

Take a look at the verbs in these two. So much of your strength as a writer depends on your choice of verbs—they are the amplifiers of language. The stronger and fresher your verbs, the more your writing crackles.

Now, you try.

DAY #6

TETRAMETER COUPLETS

This is the last day of tetrameter couplets. As always, keep your writing sense-bound, and keep your eyes open for metaphor. Set a timer and respond to the following prompts for exactly the time allotted. Use only tetrameter couplets, and vary your rhythms, using both duples and triples.

Sight Sound Taste Touch Smell Body Motion

10 minutes: Skydiving

BLEU

Fear swelling up with the pressure of air
A thousand wind fingers grasping at my loose hair
I stare down the farms, like postage stamps, scattered
The physics too real, the gravity, matter(s)
Can't find the courage, might not find the cord

Forget butterflies, these are horse-flies, swarms
Somebody's screaming, can't make out the words
The lips look like "now!"? … my vision is blurred
… then suddenly … silence … floating free
Sky … ground … air … me

SUSAN CATTANEO

Floating and flying, arms aloft
Clouds like towers, full and soft
Rush of air, lungs expand
A human umbrella with open hands
Heart like a piston, high on the speed
Race like a bullet, slice at the breeze
The bloom of the parachute pulls and billows
You touch ground, gentle as a pillow
Smiling up at the blue and the light
Like Icarus, you are born for sky and flight

Both Bleu and Susan take you right there with some lovely sense-bound writing. Look at the metaphors, "a thousand wind fingers," "the bloom of the parachute," and the simile "clouds like towers."

Your turn.

5 minutes: Rocking Chair on the Front Porch at Sunset

BLEU

Grandma's fingers stringing beans
Cicada soothing me to sleep
Fireflies blinking, honeysuckle breeze
Simple, southern, harmonies
Two crescents of wood, on older wood
This porch knows the way great-grandma stood
So I rock, slow and slower still
And hum the Lonesome Whippoorwill

CHANELLE DAVIS

Little peepers lace the pond
Sun is setting orange on blonde
Pour a wine and settle in
Toast the cool and silent wind
A rocking chair for company
He drifts inside a memory

I like the beans/sleep assonance rhyme—it doesn't lock down; rather, it relaxes the structure. Look at the rhyme breeze/harmonies, using the secondary stress *harmo**nies.*** Be careful rhyming secondary stress with primary stress: If you place the secondary stress on a stronger musical beat than the primary stress, you'll distort the natural shape of the word. The same would be true for compa**ny**/memo**ry**. For more on this, check out my "Writing Lyrics to Music" online course at Berklee College of Music, available through http://patpattison.com/patsonlinecourses.

Your turn.

DAY #7

COMMON METER

For more on common meter, look at chapters fourteen, fifteen, and eighteen in *Writing Better Lyrics,* and chapter three in *The Essential Guide to Lyric Form and Structure.*

The best way to create sections larger than couplets is to vary line length. Start with this tetrameter line:

DUM da da DUM da DUM da da DUM
Give her a chance to sing by herself

Next, add a shorter, three-stress line (trimeter), keeping the same triple feel:

DUM da da DUM da DUM da da DUM
DUM da da DUM da DUM

Give her a chance to sing by herself

Give her the room to shine

You tap your foot four times in line 1, but only three times in line 2. Your body feels the imbalance—there are some matching rhythms between line 1 and line 2, but the differing lengths of the lines causes instability, throwing the section off balance. Since you are off balance, you must continue to move forward.

Match the third line with the first line, and rhyme with it. You'll create strong expectations for a fourth line:

DUM da da DUM da DUM da da DUM
DUM da da DUM da DUM
DUM da da DUM da DUM da da DUM

Give her a chance to sing by herself
Give her the room to shine
Watch as she smiles and everyone melts

Now the pressure builds. The structure is still unstable, with its odd number of lines. Because lines 1 and 3 match, you expect something quite specific:

A fourth line to balance with an even number of lines
A line that matches the length and rhythm of line two (the odd-duck line)

Specifically, you want to hear

DUM da da DUM da DUM

giving you this section:

DUM da da DUM da DUM da da DUM
DUM da da DUM da DUM
DUM da da DUM da DUM da da DUM
DUM da da DUM da DUM

Give her a chance to sing by herself
Give her the room to shine
Watch as she smiles and everyone melts

Hearing a voice divine

You feel the resolution. It is called *common meter.* You will find it everywhere, because it, like the tetrameter couplet, fits perfectly into an eight-bar sequence.

Today you'll use common meter. You have your choice in common meter of rhyming alternate lines, abab ...

Give her a chance to sing by herself
Give her the room to shine
Watch as she smiles and everyone melts
Hearing a voice divine

or rhyming lines two and four, xaxa ...

Give her a chance to sing all alone
Give her the room to shine
Watch as she smiles and everyone melts
Hearing a voice divine

For the next two days, simply rhyme the trimeter lines. After that, you'll rhyme alternate lines.

Keep your writing sense-bound, and keep your eyes open for metaphor. As usual, set a timer and respond to the following prompts for exactly the time allotted. Use the whole time, whether you complete your final four-line section or not. Use common meter, rhyming only the trimeter lines (xaxa).

Sight Sound Taste Touch Smell Body Motion

10 minutes: Whistling

ANDREA STOLPE

Wrinkled and puckered she purses her lips
Angry and close to tears
Everyone else can whistle a tune
But she hasn't whistled in years
Airy and flimsy and flattered with spit

Forcing the air she tries
Till somebody mentions that field grass
Held with her thumbs is fine
Plucking a blade young and green
Cupping her fingers around
She strokes the air with effortless skill
Releasing a covetous sound

JESS MEIDER

Puckered and folded like a circular fan
Breath pulls in like a thread
The hollow resounds a mini wind song
Air and shape wed
Lips give birth to thin high-pitched notes
The tip of the tongue taps
Dividing the melody coming up from the throat
Mimic the bird's rap

Both rely primarily on triple meter, and work the four-stress/three-stress of common meter very well. Note that the adjacent strong stresses in Jess's "shape wed," "tongue taps," and "bird's rap" force either a musical rest or longer notes when set to music.

Your turn.

5 minutes: Falling in Love

STAN SWINIARSKI

Give me a song to remember the night
Let the candle burn low
And soon I will tell you a love that is lost
That's how these stories go
Give me the scent of magnolia trees
And sweet tea on the lawn
And soon that glass will be smellin' like bourbon
That's how fast love is gone
Give me a beauty with hazelnut eyes

And I'll tell you of promises
Like the moon smells of lilacs and fresh-cut grass
And broken dreams and wishes

ANDREA STOLPE

Streamers on bicycles ribbons on balloons
dancing on pockets of air
spinning and sailing and landing with ease
when love is everywhere

Rocky and jagged and bitter to taste
bruising and jarring the soul
cursing the life that love would touch
dying the day it goes

Stan's first four lines have only the candle to engage your senses, as opposed to Andrea, who pulls you in immediately. But when Stan hits line 5, everything starts to crackle, especially "the moon smells of lilacs and fresh-cut grass." Nice. I love how Andrea wrote opposing quatrains, as positive and negative aspects of falling in love.

Note especially Stan's rhyme promi**ses**/wi**shes**. The secondary stress *ses* against the weak syllable *shes* lets the idea float off into dreamland. There are good reasons to use less- than-perfect rhymes. They create instability, which is right on target for his piece. Open your ears and learn how and when to use your rhyme types.

Now, you try.

DAY #8

COMMON METER

Keep your writing sense-bound, and keep your eyes open for metaphor. As usual, set a timer and respond to the following prompts for exactly the time allotted. Use the whole time, whether you complete your final four-line section or not. Use common meter, rhyming only the trimeter lines (xaxa).

10 minutes: Ballerina

SARAH BRINDELL

Plastic ballerina spins
Inside my jewelry case
Twirling in her little room
Of pink sateen and lace
She dances till the song is gone
Then freezes for a while
Ripped tutu and some chipping paint
Reveal her half-gone smile
This home that once held pearls and gold
Is now an empty shell
And all her ballerina days
Are bidding their farewell

CHANELLE DAVIS

The feel of satin on her skin
It stretches shiny and tight
Rose pink to match her shoes
Sweeping to the light
And there she pauses for a moment
The people simmer down
She twirls and twirls to the orchestra
Her body floats to the ground
Lights bounce off her silky silhouette
A piece of string in the breeze
Twists and turns caught in midair
Moving graceful, free

Both paint lovely pictures. I love Sarah's music box approach, which could even be a metaphor for lost youth. And check out Chanelle's metaphor "her silky silhouette/A piece of string in the breeze." Nice.

Your turn.

5 minutes: 18-Wheeler

SUSAN CATTANEO

A farmer's tan on his left bicep
His USMC tattoo
Camel smokes in his checkered pocket
He swigs a Mountain Dew
Detroit to San José and back
He keeps those wheels a'rolling
He pushes miles between memories
To keep those ghosts from calling

SARAH BRINDELL

The flick of a lighter, the twitch of a shoulder
A man holds tight to the wheel
The revving motor, the sound of thunder
Brakes let out a squeal
High beams blind your dim-lit path
On this sweaty deserted night
No more wasted freeway drives
Where no sleep warps your sight

Nice sense-bound writing. And I love Susan's consonance rhyme rolling/calling, which creates a spooky feeling to support the trucker's flight from his memories. And Sarah's "no sleep warps your sight." With this relaxed rhyme scheme, you should be able to finish two quatrains.

Your turn.

DAY #9

COMMON METER

Keep your writing sense-bound, and keep your eyes open for metaphor. As usual, set a timer and respond to the following prompts for exactly the time allotted. Use the whole time, whether you complete your final four-line section or not. Use common meter, rhyming both your tetrameter and trimeter lines (abab).

Sight Sound Taste Touch Smell Body Motion

10 minutes: Ocean Waves

SCARLET KEYS

Salty fingers reach and pull
Bring your tired feet
Bring your hungry lonely fools
Here to walk my beach
They'll love the way the sun sinks low
And slows the city pace
I'll send a gentle wind to blow
The curls from her face
Run through my water jump in the waves
Let me salt your skin
Dip her body from her waist
Here's where love begins
Trace her name in the sandy shore
Draw a heart with a shell
Take her where she's ...

CHANELLE DAVIS

Ocean waves come rushing in
Over the sandy beach
Stop to touch your summer skin
The water licks our feet
Dogs are chasing driftwood sticks
Swimming for the prize
When he's done he shakes and flicks
There's water in our eyes
Chocolate ice cream and waffle cones
Cooling on my tongue

Afternoon sun warms my bones
Salt air fills my lungs

Look at the point of view in Scarlet's piece. It's as though the waves themselves are talking, and the result is lots of energy. That's the power of direct address (see chapter ten, *Writing Better Lyrics*). In both Scarlet's and Chanelle's poems, the language is very active, which is partially a result of direct address and how it presents the opportunity to give commands with verbs, the amplifiers of language:

Bring your tired feet
Bring your hungry lonely fools ...
Run through my water jump in the waves
Let me salt your skin
Dip her body from her waist ...
Trace her name in the sandy shore
Draw a heart with a shell
Take her where she's ...
Stop to touch your summer skin

Your turn.

5 minutes: Magnifying Glass

ANDREA STOLPE

Pungent sickly crackling smoke
of frantic frying ants
Floated up from the beam that shone
through deathly convex glass
I stood and smoothed my wrinkled dress
and kicked the sand a bit
A stain on the concrete was all that was left
that summer my parents split

SUSAN CATTANEO

Giant spider legs wiggle
Eyes the size of boulders

Mary Whitman starts to giggle
Her science teacher scolds her
Petrie glasses growing mold
A skeleton hangs from a hook
Johnny Duncan picks his nose
While he doodles faces in his book
The tang of sulfur, boiling beakers
Test tubes in a row
Pencils scribbling, untied sneakers
Hair wrapped in a bow

I love Andrea's punch line, especially after the cruel, macabre picture she paints. The ants are a wonderful metaphor for the anger and pain inside the child. Susan, as usual, draws the reader in with strong sense-bound language. I was back in Mr. Conroy's science class instantly.

Both handle the tighter rhyme constraints with aplomb.

Now, you try.

DAY #10

COMMON METER

Keep your writing sense-bound, and keep your eyes open for metaphor. As usual, set a timer and respond to the following prompts for exactly the time allotted. Use the whole time, whether you complete your final four-line section or not. Use common meter, again rhyming both your tetrameter and trimeter lines (abab).

Sight Sound Taste Touch Smell Body Motion

10 minutes: Slot Machine

STAN SWINIARSKI

The land of the smokers' last revenge
Lights flash, bells are ringing

Like a siren that calls my last dime to its death
Let me hear that temptress singing
My arm's getting weary with every pull
Buttons have no hold on me
The lights flash and give me its promising thrill
I will have my victory
Blue-hairs and blue-collars standing in line
Hoping for a loose machine
I gallantly give up my space this time, so
Someone else could live this dream

SUSAN CATTANEO

She's parked at the one armed bandit
Her quarters in a plastic cup
Sipping her fifth gin and tonic
Hoping for lady luck
Her hair's a hornet's nest of blue
Eyes rheumy with the smoke
She's humming a dirty little tune
A cross gleaming at her throat
The jangle of the coins is heaven falling
And silence is hell on earth
She lives for the thrill that fortune's calling
Her winnings define her worth
The carousel music enfolds her
She's drunk on neon light
This jackpot hope will hold her
Till day runs into night

Both of these take me to the casino. I especially like Stan's use of the organic (body) sense: "My arm's getting weary with every pull." Note also the consonance rhyme pull/thrill. Susan's bandit/tonic is interesting—dit/ic is a weak syllable family rhyme, and ban/ton is a consonance rhyme. They also match shapes, moving stressed to unstressed.

You try.

5 minutes: Deep-Sea Diver

ADRIANA DUARTE

You're a lonely deep sea diver
Always wanting more
Just another tipsy driver
Serve another pour

CHANELLE DAVIS

My flashlight is a lonely moon
Shining in the dark
The ocean sings a silent tune
A night without its stars
Maybe they are buried here
Somewhere in the sand
Slow your breathing, lose the fear
Underwater man

I love Adriana's metaphor: a drunk, diving deep into a sea of alcohol. In second person, Chanelle puts you immediately underwater with "my flashlight is a lonely moon." Metaphors abound. Her last two lines are commands, turning first person into second person—making it feel like he's talking to himself.

Your turn.

DAY #11

TETRAMETER AND PENTAMETER

Today you'll work in an extended form, in six-line units rhyming aabccb, with tetrameter couplets and pentameter following lines.

As you've already seen, tetrameter couplets subdivide into units of two, creating an unrelenting march of the smallest sections possible. This time, create a section that doesn't end until the final line. It'll feel better; more interesting.

Start here:

Tumbling and tumbling, boulders and rocks
Fallen away from the red mountain top

But now try throwing the tetrameter couplet off balance by inserting a five-stress (pentameter) line:

Tumbling and tumbling, boulders and rocks	4-stress
Fallen away from the red mountain top	4-stress
Dúst on the hórses, spréading all óver the town	5-stress

You can feel the IOU. The five-stress pentameter line creates a push forward, not only because it creates an odd number of lines, but because it doesn't rhyme either. Now add another tetrameter couplet:

Tumbling and tumbling, boulders and rocks
Fallen away from the red mountain top
Dust on the horses, spreading all over the town
Color of blood, the color of pain
Some of these children won't breathe again

You can feel the urgency. The structure is asking you to match line line 3, both in length (pentameter) and rhyme.

Like this:

Tumbling and tumbling, boulders and rocks
Fallen away from the red mountain top
Dust on the horses, spreading all over the town
Color of blood, the color of pain
Some of these children won't breathe again
Dúst like a ghóst cloud swírling and púlling you dówn

Of course, there are rhyme variations possible. What if the tetrameter lines didn't rhyme?

Tumbling and tumbling, boulders and shale
Fallen away from the red mountain top
Dust on the horses, spreading all over the town
Color of blood, the color of soot

Some of these children won't breathe again
Dust like a ghost cloud swirling and pulling you down

Now the structure feels more relaxed. The push forward is milder, generated only by line length, since the first rhyme doesn't occur until the very last syllable.

Today you'll rhyme your ten-minute piece aabccb, and your five-minute piece xxaxxa, following the model:

Tetrameter	a
Tetrameter	a
Pentameter	b
Tetrameter	c
Tetrameter	c
Pentameter	b

Keep your writing sense-bound, and keep your eyes open for metaphor. As usual, set a timer and respond to the following prompts for exactly the time allotted. Use the whole time, whether or not you complete your final section. Don't panic. It'll be challenging, but fun.

Sight **Sound** **Taste** **Touch** **Smell** **Body** **Motion**

10 minutes: War Zone (aabccb)

SUSAN CATTANEO

Ravaged concrete lies in rubble
Sirens screaming, the town's in trouble
Airplanes buzz like gnats through open skies
Duck and cover, hide your fear
Soldiers march, the tanks are near
Creeping over the pitted land like flies
Bombs sing through smoke and air
Dropping death with utmost care
The beast of war is here and on the prowl
Savage talons tear and claw
Wings of steel, a gaping maw

The fearful earth shudders as it howls

ROB GILES

Black and white pictures, darkening blood
Piles of mothers and babies in mud
Prints, they float like bodies face up in the fixer
CNN news crews laugh by their tents
Meters away, the dead broken and bent
Ghosts from a war zone crying thru 8x10 pictures

Note how Rob uses his cc lines to shift the focus to the reporters. It's an effective use of form that takes advantage of the change in rhyme sound to support the change in perspective. Susan does the same thing in lines 4 and 5, introducing a command to shift the tone at the same time the new rhyme sound appears. Form is a road map. It tells you where to go.

There are effective metaphor and simile in each one, too, as well as provocative sense-bound language.

Note how much content their rhymes contain:

Rubble	Blood
Trouble	Mud
Skies	Fixer
Fear	Tents
Near	Bent
Flies	Pictures
Air	
Care	
Prowl	
Claw	
Maw	
Howls	

You get so much of the story just from the rhyme positions! The rhyming positions are in the spotlights. Use them. (See my *Essential Guide to Rhyming* on this point.)

Try it out.

5 minutes: Wildflowers (xxaxxa)

CHANELLE DAVIS

Wildflowers growing in the neighbour's field
Cupcake sprinkles in the summer green
Bees hover and roll in their sticky pollen
Jump the fence to pick a few
Bunch them up in my old shirt
Quickly home before they know I stole 'em

SUSAN CATTANEO

Clover droops its purple head
Daisies dancing in the breeze
Clouds are skipping through an ocean sky
The meadow dappled emerald green
Bees hover like helicopters
Summer gives a small contented sigh

Whatever motion there is comes from line lengths matching and unmatching, not from rhyme. These sections feel like they float with only rhythm driving the bus, since we don't hear a rhyme until the end. It seems appropriate for the dreamy subject, *wildflowers*. Chanelle's consonance rhyme pollen/stole 'em refuses to close the dreaming down. Even Susan's perfect rhyme just barely gets the screen door closed. Both create wonderful pictures and buttress them with metaphor.

Again, note how much of the story is told from the end-line positions.

Your turn.

DAY #12

COMMON METER AND PENTAMETER

One thing you'll notice about rhyming aabccb: The couplets still produce a stop sign, especially the first couplet (aa). Rather than letting your section subdivide at the end of line 2, try creating a section that doesn't end until the final line.

Start with the two unequal first lines of common meter:

Tumbling and tumbling, boulders and rocks
The color of blood and pain

Now, instead of continuing the common meter, insert a pentameter line:

Tumbling and tumbling, boulders and rocks
The color of blood and pain
Dust on the horses, spreading all over the town

Though there are no rhymes (yet), you can feel the instability and the need to keep moving forward. Try a tetrameter line, rhyming with line 1:

	STRESSES	RHYME SCHEME
Tumbling and tumbling, boulders and rocks	4	a
The color of blood and pain	3	b
Dust on the horses, spreading all over the town	5	c
Fallen away from the red mountaintop	4	a

You've matched line 1, so now you've raised expectations that the sequence will continue, will push forward:

	STRESSES	RHYME SCHEME
Tumbling and tumbling, boulders and rocks	4	a
The color of blood and pain	3	b
Dust on the horses, spreading all over the town	5	c
Fallen away from the red mountaintop	4	a
On children who won't breathe again	3	b

Now you've got to complete the series:

	STRESSES	RHYME SCHEME
Tumbling and tumbling, boulders and rocks	4	a
The color of blood and pain	3	b

Dust on the horses, spreading all over the town	5	c
Fallen away from the red mountaintop	4	a
On children who won't breathe again	3	b
Dust like a ghost cloud swirling and pulling them down	5	c

Again, you have options with the rhyme scheme. Here are two, the first, unrhyming lines 1, 2, 4, and 5 to create an xxaxxa rhyme scheme:

STRESSES		**RHYME SCHEME**
Tumbling and tumbling, boulders and rocks	4	x
The color of blood and shale	3	x
Dust on the horses, spreading all over the town	5	a
Fallen away from the red mountainside	4	x
On children who won't breathe again	3	x
Dust like a ghost cloud swirling and pulling them down	5	a

Now the long third and sixth pentameter lines provide the main glue, creating a six-line section that keeps moving all the way to the end.

Of course, you can use more rhymes, too. You can rhyme the second and fourth common meter lines, creating an xabxab rhyme scheme:

STRESSES		**RHYME SCHEME**
Tumbling and tumbling, boulders and rocks	4	x
The color of blood and pain	3	a
Dust on the horses, spreading all over the town	5	b
Fallen away from the red mountainside	4	x
On children who won't breathe again	3	a
Dust like a ghost cloud swirling and pulling them down	5	b

I like options. They allow you to match the mood of the section—tight or loose.

Today you'll work with common meter and pentameter, creating six-line sections that move forward until the end.

Keep your writing sense-bound, and keep your eyes open for metaphor. As usual, set a timer and respond to the following prompts for exactly the time allotted. Use the whole time, whether or not you complete your final section.

Rhyme your ten-minute piece abcabc, and your five-minute piece xxaxxa.

Sight Sound Taste Touch Smell Body Motion

10 minutes: Morning Walk (abcabc)

STAN SWINIARSKI

Sneakers that patter on fresh morning sidewalks
The rhythm starts the day
Smells of wet grass, sprinklers wetting the greens
Peaceful as dreaming, the morning bird's talks
Lead me on my way
Feeling the sky's welcoming yawn to me

Ladies pass by with their gossip and iPods
The colors that I see
Bright-colored sweatsuits in their full morning bloom
Men in their khakis being led by their dogs
Greeting every tree
They will be off to their workday very soon

ANDREA STOLPE

Walking alone down the matted path
I weave a trail through the wood
Listening closely to the sound of my breath, exhaling
Bundled and warm in a fleece jacket
I gently untie my hood
As the sweet scent of poplars takes me away, sailing

As opposed to yesterday's tetrameter/pentameter pieces, see how the shorter second line pushes forward without the help of rhyme. If fact, you don't hear the first rhyme until the end of line 4. In Andrea's piece, path/jacket is a partial rhyme—only the stressed syllables (path/jack) rhyme while an unstressed syllable (et) hangs over.

Both pieces take you on a nice walk with their sense-bound language.

Now, you do it.

5 minutes: Traffic Cop (xxaxxa)

SUSAN CATTANEO

At the intersection of Bow and First
He's Moses parting seas
A prophet of the asphalt, shining black with tar
In orange vest and polished boots
He preens and strikes a pose
His hand conducts a symphony of cars

CHANELLE DAVIS

He waves his arms left and right
Blasts his whistle and frowns
The morning traffic slowly stops and starts
Each car like a drop of blood
Pumped down the plastic tube
Into the city, into its beating heart

Even without rhymes in the tetrameter and trimeter lines, the line lengths push forward pretty strongly. For a deeper look, see chapter sixteen, "Understanding Motion," in *Writing Better Lyrics*. It's true, however, that without the xxaxxa rhyme scheme relaxes the forward push.

Check out the metaphors in Susan's piece, and the simile in Chanelle's.

Your turn.

DAY #13

COMMON METER AND PENTAMETER

Again today you'll work with common meter and pentameter, creating six-line sections that move forward until the end.

Keep your writing sense-bound, and keep your eyes open for metaphor. As usual, set a timer and respond to the following prompts for exactly the time allotted. Use the whole time, whether or not you complete your final section.

Rhyme your ten-minute piece abcabc, and your five-minute piece xabxab.

Sight Sound Taste Touch Smell Body Motion

10 minutes: Trash Collector (abcabc)

STAN SWINIARSKI

Rancid old salads and musty wine bottles
He don't mind the stuff
He's got a pension that many folks would kill for
Waterlogged cans weigh him down as he toddles
Toward the waiting truck
Just ten more years and he's heading for the shore

Some yearn for pride and some work for status
That don't light his fire
He's got two kids in college, doing well
The flies buzz and they swarm but it doesn't matter
'Cause time is on his side
In the end he knows his time will tell

Being a surgeon was not in the cards
He puts his family first
Seeing them happy quenches this man's thirst
Some folks may say that his life is too hard
Covered in grime and dirt
But this man know's what it all is worth

SUSAN CATTANEO

Rumbling, lumbering down the street
Brakes squealing loud

A metal armored tank that's stuffed with trash
Smelling, sweltering, summer heat
Gunk, rancid and foul
Dripping on the asphalt like a rash

Bottles, cans, jelly jars
Newspapers stacked like towers
Last night's chicken bones and totems
A headless doll, crayon-scarred
A torn skirt of flowers
A letter swearing promises now broken

Everybody's got their secrets
Toss them in the can
Neighbors hide behind their shuttered shades
It can't be fixed, so just don't keep it
Hearts and hope be damned
Throw them out and watch the memories fade

In Stan's third stanza, notice how the duplication of the rhyme sounds first/thirst/dirt/worth works against the motion created by the line lengths, somewhat confusing the issue with conflicting road signs.

I like Stan's portrait of the trash collector and Susan's lists, especially: "A torn skirt of flowers" and "A letter swearing promises now broken."

Both pieces use sense-bound language effectively, provoking images of the weekly trash collection. I can hear the garbage truck coming.

Your turn.

5 minutes: Mowing the Lawn (xabxab)

CHANELLE DAVIS

Up and down my little lawn
I push for even lines

In my tight black singlet, cut-off denim jeans
A deafening buzz fills the air
Snowfreeze clouds melt in the sky
Slashing through the clumps of luscious green

SUSAN CATTANEO

His broad, brown back is stooped
A war of work in his eyes
Fighting the mower with taut and angled shoulders
Carving green in pretty rows
Perfectly aligned
Machine machete, fallen green soldiers

With this rhyme scheme, you don't hear the first rhyme until the end of line 5, which adds some push for the final rhyme. The line lengths are doing the heavy lifting again, creating the forward push. Both line length and rhyme are traffic cops, but line length has a higher rank—captain, as opposed to sergeant.

Your turn.

DAY #14

UNSTABLE STRUCTURE: ABBA

Wow! Day fourteen and you're still here. Good for you. Today you'll work with an unstable structure, one that will help support lyric ideas in the unstable camp—loss, heartbreak, hope, dreaming, etc.

Start with the first two lines of common meter:

	STRESSES	RHYME SCHEME
Tumbling and tumbling, boulders and rocks	4	a
The color of blood and pain	3	b

Now, instead of matching line 1, match line 2 and rhyme it:

	STRESSES	RHYME SCHEME
Tumbling and tumbling, boulders and rocks	4	a

The color of blood and pain	3	b
Of children who won't breathe again	3	b

Even with the rhyme, the structure feels a little funny. You feel like there might be more coming, but you have no idea what it could be. It's unstable. For more on this point, take a look at my analysis of the second verse of "Between Fathers and Sons" in chapter three of my *Essential Guide to Lyric Form and Structure.*

Without the rhyme, the feeling of suspension is even more obvious:

	STRESSES	RHYME SCHEME
Tumbling and tumbling, boulders and rocks	4	x
The color of blood and shale	3	x
Of children who won't breathe again	3	x

Either way, this third line fails to create strong expectations. The reader certainly doesn't expect a match of line 1. It might be tempting to try it, but it doesn't really balance things, since it reverses the sequence:

	STRESSES	RHYME SCHEME
Tumbling and tumbling, boulders and rocks	4	a
The color of blood and pain	3	b
Of children who won't breathe again	3	b
Stolen away by the red mountain top	4	a

Today you'll work in this abba structure. It creates an interesting feeling of floating, and by itself, will probably pull you into more unstable, dreamy places.

Keep your writing sense-bound, and keep your eyes open for metaphor. As usual, set a timer and respond to the following prompts for exactly the time allotted. Use the whole time, whether or not you complete your final section.

Rhyme your ten-minute piece abba, and your five-minute piece axxa. Use tetrameter lines for the outside lines, 1 and 4, trimeter lines for the inside lines, 2 and 3.

10 minutes: Cloudy Day (abba)

CHANELLE DAVIS

Cloudy days remind me of you
We didn't feel the cold
And thirty seemed so old
Empty pockets and nothing to lose

Drinking wine and playing cards
Pretending to fall asleep
I would watch you breathe
You were tangled up in my heart

Slowly all the love unwinds
Threads and nothing more
Piled up on the floor
Left from once upon a time

SUSAN CATTANEO

Wispy, moping, low and gray
They huddle close to the ground
Scowling ether frowns
They wander listless, clump then fray

Cranky clouds throw a fit
Thundering and whining
Eyes full of lightning
Spitting rain from snarling lips

The sun comes with mother arms
Cuddles gray to white
Closing stormy eyes
Calming tempers with her warming heart

Pretty floaty stuff. Check out Chanelle's extended thread metaphor, beginning with *tangled*. And Susan's extended metaphor personifying the clouds, beginning with *moping*.

Now watch what happens if you turn this abba sequence into equal length tetrameter lines:

The sun comes with mother arms
Cuddles gray to pearly white
Finally closing stormy eyes
Calming tempers with her warming heart

This is called an "In Memoriam" quatrain, after a poem of that title by Alfred, Lord Tennyson. It was a poem mourning the death of a friend, and because the rhyme scheme's unstable nature was so perfectly appropriate for the subject matter, the name stuck to both the rhyme scheme and the quatrain.

I encourage you to experiment with this equal-line-length version of abba, but for now, use tetrameter lines for your outside lines, trimeter lines for your inside lines.

Try it now.

5 minutes: Sleeping Late (axxa)

SARAH BRINDELL

Float on a steady stream
Forfeit all your chores
Broken alarm clock
Slip inside your heavy dream

Lids barred at your eyelash seam
Overlook the day
Shades fake the time
The bed holds a broken machine

SUSAN CATTANEO

Yawning wide as an open field

Stretching in the lazy sun
Skies melt like ice
The August sun is ripe and peeled

These really float. The interruption of motion that happens in the abba version of the rhyme scheme does not happen here.

Both Sarah and Susan set us a'dreaming. A lovely finish for Challenge #4.

And now it's your turn. Good luck!

AFTERWORD

Of course, you know you haven't finished. You've really only started. You now have the focus and the discipline that makes writing such a joyful experience. You can begin doing your work with new skills, new eyes and ears.

Do your morning object writing; you have so many variations on it, you can stay excited to see what your writer will come up with next. I'd tell you to do metaphor exercises on a regular basis, but it's probably too late for that. Metaphor should be such a part of your bloodstream by now that the exercises have become your normal way of seeing.

You should now be faster with your rhythms and more attentive to rhyme and rhyme structures. That'll make brainstorming ideas more fun, since now you can do it while you're trying out rhythms and rhymes—working simultaneously on all three levels. You'll get farther faster.

If you did the challenges with friends, keep it up. Meet once a week to do object writing and metaphor exercises. Gillian Welch did, for 2½ years, and meeting with a group of Berklee alumni, culminating in her publishing deal and close behind, her record deal. She still does her object writing. She found her voice, big time.

Mostly, congratulations for finishing. I hope this was useful and served your writing needs. I had a great time putting it together. I had such wonderful help.

My deepest gratitude to all my contributors.

Pat Pattison
July 25, 2011

TO THE CONTRIBUTORS:

I am honored that you, and so many others, stepped up to the plate and submitted your work. I had a marvelous time going through all the entries, as many as forty for some prompts—I'm grateful to Clare McLeod for helping me work through them.

I learned a lot, reading your work. When you write from your senses, when you search for metaphor, clichés and generic writing melt away into something beautiful and compelling. It comes from a real place in you. And so, opens a real place in me. That's why it's so much fun.

It's wonderful to get to know you.

SHANE ADAMS, *Nashville TN*
SAM ALESSI, *Idaho Falls ID*
SUSAN ANDERS, *Nashville TN*
GREG BECKER, *Nashville TN*
DAVEY BEIGE, *Auckland NZ*
BLEU, *Los Angeles CA*
NELSON BOGART, *New York NY*
CATHY BRETTELL, *Denver CO*
HOLLY BRETTELL, *Denver CO*
SARAH BRINDELL, *San Francisco CA*
MEGAN BURTT, *Denver CO*
SUSAN CATTANEO, *Boston MA*
ANTHONY CESERI, *Red Bank NJ*
KRISTIN CIFELLI, *Boston MA*
KEPPIE COUTTS, *Sydney Australia*
CHRIS COWAN, *Austin TX*
CHANELLE DAVIS, *Melbourne Australia*
ADRIANA DUARTE, *Lisbon Portugal*
ADAM FARR, *Granada Spain*
ROB GILES, *Los Angeles CA*
JOY GORA, *Longmeadow MA*
EMILY GREENE, *New York NY*
ANN HALVORSEN, *San Francisco CA*
CAROLINE HARVEY, *Boston MA*
BONNIE HAYES, *San Francisco CA*
IAN HENCHY, *Cape Cod MA*
MATT K *(prefers to remain anonymous)*
SCARLET KEYS, *Portsmouth NH*
JOANNA LEIGH, *Newcastle NSW, Australia*
SYLVIE LEWIS, *London UK*
KAMI LYLE, *Harwich MA*
LINDA M, *Toronto Canada*
CLARE MCLEOD, *North Hampton NH*
MO MCMORROW, *Austin TX*
JESS MEIDER, *Beijing China*
JAMES MERENDA, *Brooklyn NY*
NICK MILLER, *Sydney Australia*
KAZ MITCHELL, *Melbourne Australia*
SARAH MOUNT, *Boston MA*
TAMI NEILSON, *Auckland NZ*
LEORA NOSKO, *Louisville KY*
REBECCA OLMSTED, *Berlin Germany*

JOHN O'SHAUGHNESSY, *Lake Cathie Australia*

CHARLOTTE PENCE, *Knoxville TN*

PAUL PENTON, *Melbourne Australia*

DEBORAH QUILTER, *Melbourne Australia*

TASLEEM RAJWANI, *Vancouver British Columbia Canada*

BEN ROMANS, *Los Angeles CA*

LEORA SALO, *Houston TX*

CATRINA SEIFFERT, *Melbourne Australia*

MICHAEL SHORR, *Taos NM*

AMY SPEACE, *Nashville TN*

ANDREA STOLPE, *Los Angeles CA*

MANUEL STÜBINGER, *Kulmbach Germany*

STAN SWINIARSKI, *Boston MA*

SHIRLEY TO, *Chino Hills CA*

NICHOLAS TOZIER, *Jefferson ME*

TANJA WARD, *Washington DC*

GILLIAN WELCH, *Nashville TN*

SCOTT WILKINSON, *Birmingham MI*

CHARLIE WORSHAM, *Nashville TN*

THE CONTRIBUTORS TALK ABOUT THE CHALLENGES

Pat Pattison is the writing teacher I've been long praying for and his writing exercises are nothing short of revolutionary. I'm almost embarrassed to say that after over a decade of professional creative writing I don't think I ever fully understood the function and craft of metaphor until diving in to the writing challenges of *Songwriting Without Boundaries*. With the elegant flair of a wonderfully mad scientist, Pat pulls the best out of artists and empowers us to make the work we've always wanted to make. The poetry I've produced since investing in Pat's teaching has been some of the liveliest, most powerful, and most published work of my career so far. His smart, inventive, cut-to-the-chase instruction has been the necessary overhaul for my whole creative life; the very core of my writing practice has been revamped and infused with new, lustrous lifeblood. His books sit open on my desk, dog-eared and well worn.

—CAROLINE HARVEY, PROFESSIONAL POET,
FEATURED ON HBO'S *DEF POETRY JAM*

The last time I made four new songs in a month that I liked was a long time ago. Having to work the challenges opens a gate into a garden where I can get pleasure out of using language again. Noticing connections between things is like a beautiful tree in that garden, with abundant fruit.

One more thing; I have always found as a teacher that getting certain students to "get" metaphor was difficult; it sort of seemed like one either has the knack or not. But I feel like Pat's approach may be one of the best methods of teaching writers to use figurative language I've encountered; and in fact, it may be the only one. I can't wait to use this book in my classes as well as in my own work.

—BONNIE HAYES, SONGWRITER ("HAVE A HEART," BONNIE RAITT),
TEACHER, SAN FRANCISCO, CA

I never realized how restricted and confined my lyrics were until I started doing Pat's exercises. The exercises opened the door to a vast expanse of lyrical options that I had rarely tapped into. The depth and interest of my lyrics improved greatly even after the first few days of doing the exercises. My brain was forced out of its routine and strengthened new muscles of imagination that will become the new default setting for all my writing to come. It's too easy to become complacent in our writing and important for us all to constantly challenge ourselves in the way that Pat has shown us here. The methods he teaches in this book are effective and lasting.

—GREG BECKER, SONGWRITER (CARRIE UNDERWOOD, RASCAL FLATTS), NASHVILLE, TN

In the middle of working on these challenges I left for a writing/ recording trip to Mexico to work on my new record ... so I sort of had an immediate test of the effect of these exercise. It was pretty amazing. My writing didn't "change" per se—it was still me, working in my normal style, but, everything came faster, and more fluidly. Some of the ideas almost seemed to fall out fully formed. Above all—I think that's the magic of this book—it preps your brain to be a better you.

—BLEU, RECORDING ARTIST, SONGWRITER, PRODUCER, LOS ANGELES, CA

Pat's lessons gave me a voice so many years ago, and many of those tools I still use almost daily. But when I was given a new assignment, I was so intimidated, I almost couldn't bring myself to try them. Would I be able to meet his expectations? Or mine? Once I dove in I quickly realized that, once again, I was going to be led across the dance floor to where the lights don't shine, that I would improve in places that I didn't know I had places. Pat and his challenges have a way of saying "Psst, come here, back behind these familiar words ... I wanna show you something ..." And from there, an unknown vista comes into focus and changes your perspective forever.

—ROB GILES, SONGWRITER, RECORDING ARTIST (THE RESCUES), LOS ANGELES, CA

Before the challenges, I feared metaphor. If one crept into my song I probably wouldn't have known about it. Pat's exercises exposed metaphor for what it is—one of the most important and exciting tools a writer can possess. It flicked a switch in my brain, and suddenly I could see metaphors everywhere! Overnight my songs became more original and memorable because I could express my ideas in a unique way. I now have the ability to paint pictures with my lyrics, and show rather than tell by using sense bound language.

Writing every day felt great. Even if just for 15-20min, I was doing my job and becoming a better songwriter. Each challenge built nicely into the next, and before I knew it I was using metaphor, sense bound language, line length AND throwing in rhymes! This is where the magic happens. It has definitely taken my writing to the next level—and I had fun doing it.

—CHANELLE DAVIS, SONGWRITER, RECORDING ARTIST, MELBOURNE, AUSTRALIA

Ever since day one of object writing, Pat's never-ending coaching, wisdom, exercises, and crafting have always provided one of the most important responsibilities as a songwriter: awareness. Awareness of all possibilities, and what can carve deeper into the listener's mind.

—BEN ROMANS, SONGWRITER, RECORDING ARTIST (THE CLICK FIVE) LOS ANGELES, CA

The object writing challenge for me started out as written fragments of sentiment and awkwardness, which had a habit of splattering untidily as the timer ticked away. As the days passed, my writing settled into strangely cozy corners of storytelling. By the end of the challenge my writing was sitting in the sunshine in a leafy valley, dusted with a frankness uncovered during this wonderful writing practice. I recommend object writing wholeheartedly, to all writers.

—DEBORAH QUILTER, SONGWRITER, MELBOURNE, AUSTRALIA

Oh, I loved these challenges! They wake you up creatively so that you're viewing the world in terms of metaphor, looking for just the right verb or noun that paints the picture you've got in your head. I found that they were the perfect exercises to do before actually writing a song—kind of like a great mental warm up before the marathon.

I also found that working in meter really started me focusing on strong vs. weak words and playing with duple and triple feel in lyrics. When you add in the power of making sonic connections through rhyme, you really get a great sense of how meter and rhyme can hold a section together. In my opinion, these exercises are a must for every songwriter.

—SUSAN CATTANEO, ARTIST, SONGWRITING FACULTY, BERKLEE COLLEGE OF MUSIC

The object writing challenge is a guaranteed solution to writer's block! It is a multi-purpose tool that invited me to silence my inner critic and jump into the limitless potential of original sensory images that only exist within me.

The progressive nature of the challenge (moving from who, to where, etc.) encouraged me to focus on the juicy details in each category in order to paint a picturesque scene that truly invites someone to sit down and listen.

The different time lengths in the challenge taught me that those jewels patiently waiting to be found can just as quickly rise to the top if I was writing for 10 minutes or 90 seconds. It is a dependable skill that can be fired up at any time in the songwriting process.

Doing the challenge also resulted in a wellspring of fresh song titles, verses, and choruses that I never would have realized without the technique.

I would absolutely recommend the process to any songwriter. It is especially motivating completing the challenge within a community of other writers.

—JOY GORA, SONGWRITER, LONGMEADOW, MA

INDEX

Adams, Shane, 14-15, 19-20, 181, 218
adjective-noun collisions exercise
  See also adjective-noun collisions exercise prompts
adjective-noun collisions exercise prompts
  blackened autumn, 56-57
  blackened funeral, 53-54
  fallen carburetor, 54
  fallen funeral, 57
  fevered carburetor, 58
  fevered handkerchief, 55
  lonely handkerchief, 56
  lonely moonlight, 52-53
  smooth autumn, 54-55
  smooth moonlight, 58
  See also adjective-noun collisions exercise prompts
adjectives, 50, 51, 52, 59, 65, 67, 89, 91, 92, 93, 94, 95, 97, 106, 171
  See also adjective-noun collisions exercise; finding adjectives from nouns exercise; finding nouns from adjectives exercise
adverbs, 51, 59, 171
Alessi, Sam, 13-14, 218
American Hunger, 105
Anders, Susan, 30, 218
Aristotle, 51
Arnold, Matthew, 5
articles, 172, 173
Barnhill, Greg, 100
Becker, Greg, 54, 55, 56, 78-79, 85, 86, 120, 122, 124, 218, 221
Beige, Davey, 218
"Between Fathers and Sons," 213
Bleu, 58, 183, 184-186, 188-189, 218, 221
Blink, 24
Bogart, Nelson, 22, 41, 218
Brettell, Cathy, 7-8, 10-11, 12, 218
Brettell, Holly, 31, 218
Brindell, Sarah, 152-154, 178, 195, 196, 215, 216, 218
Burtt, Megan, 121-122, 218
Butler, Samuel, 98
Card, Orson Scott, 49
Cattaneo, Susan, 11, 14, 15, 17, 21, 22, 52, 53, 54, 58, 60, 61, 62, 63, 65, 66, 69, 70, 71-72, 73, 74, 75, 76, 78, 80, 81, 83, 84, 86-87, 92, 93, 94, 97, 102, 103, 114, 117, 126, 130-131, 134-135, 137-138, 158-159, 177-178, 180-181, 189, 196, 198-199, 200, 203-204, 205, 209, 210-211, 212, 214, 215-216, 218, 223
Ceseri, Anthony, 22, 37-38, 218
challenges, writing. *See specific writing challenges, exercises, and prompts*
Chekhov, Anton, 4
Cifelli, Kristin, 63, 78, 79, 83, 87, 90, 93, 95, 103, 218
Coleridge, Samuel Taylor, 98
common meter, 169, 192, 212
  See also common meter exercise; common meter couplets; common meter couplets and pentameter lines exercise
common meter exercise, 190-201
  See also common meter exercise prompts
common meter exercise prompts
  ballerina, 195
  deep-sea diver, 201
  18-wheeler, 196
  falling in love, 193-194
  magnifying glass, 198-199
  ocean waves, 197-198

slot machine, 199-200
whistling, 192-193
common meter couplets, 205
See also common meter couplets and pentameter lines exercise
common meter couplets and pentameter lines exercise, 205-212
See also common meter couplets and pentameter lines exercise prompts
common meter couplets and pentameter lines exercise prompts
morning walk, 208
mowing the lawn, 211-212
traffic cop, 209
trash collector, 210
compound words, 172
conjunctions, 172, 173
couplets. *See* common meter couplets; common meter couplets and pentameter lines exercise; tetrameter couplets; tetrameter couplets and pentameter lines exercise; tetrameter couplets exercise
Coutts, Keppie, 60, 127-128, 182-183, 185, 186, 218
Cowan, Chris, 47, 218
Davis, Chanelle, 29-30, 33, 34, 35, 36, 37, 38, 39, 40-44, 53, 54-55, 57, 62, 68-69, 72, 73, 74, 76, 77, 82, 86, 87, 90, 91, 92-93, 94, 96, 97, 102, 103, 117, 118, 147-148, 151-152, 162, 175-176, 179, 183, 184, 189-190, 195, 197-198, 201, 205, 209, 211-212, 214, 215, 218, 222
diatonic relationship, 49, 88
direct address, 139, 140, 198
"Dover Beach," 5
Duarte, Adriana, 201, 218
duplo meter, 169
"East Coker," 1
Eliot, T.S., 1
"Essay on Criticism, An," 168
Essential Guide to Lyric Form and Structure, 190, 213
Essential Guide to Rhyming, 179, 204
exercises, writing. *See specific writing challenges, exercises, and prompts*
expressed identity, 50-51, 77, 98, 112, 129, 157, 186
forms, 77
layers of, 79-80
second form of, 79, 86, 111, 138
third form of, 82, 87
See also expressed identity exercises
expressed identity exercises, 77-87
finding nouns from nouns, 84-87
noun-noun collisions, 77-84
See also expressed identity exercises prompts
expressed identity exercises prompts
the captain is summer, 83
a cargo ship is a wince, 81-82
cathedral is ___, 86-87
an evening is a poem, 82-83
a Frisbee is a zipper, 78-79
maple tree is ___, 85
a poem is an evening, 79-80
policeman is ___, 87
a restaurant is a wineglass, 80-81
summer is the captain, 80
sunrise is ___, 86
traffic is ___, 85-86
a wince is a cargo ship, 78
a wineglass is a restaurant, 84
a zipper is a Frisbee, 82
Farr, Adam, 13, 14, 20, 36, 218
Faulkner, William, 105, 106
feminine line endings, 178
feminine rhymes, 185, 187
finding adjectives from nouns exercise, 63-66
See *also* finding adjectives from nouns exercise prompts
finding adjectives from nouns exercise prompts
___ cottage, 64-65
___ furnace, 63-64
___ ghost, 66
___ hope, 65-66
___ midnight, 64
finding linking qualities exercises
moving both directions, 158-167
working one direction, 143-158
See also finding linking qualities exercises prompts
finding linking qualities exercises prompts
afternoon nap, 150-154
magnifying glass, 143-146
sailboat, 161-164
swimming hole, 146-150
traffic cop, 154-158
vacation, 164-167
wheelchair, 158-161
finding nouns from adjectives exercise, 59-62
See also finding nouns from adjectives exercise prompts
finding nouns from adjectives exercise prompts
angry ___, 59-60
boastful ___, 60
careful ___, 61
dark ___, 61-62
enthusiastic ___, 62

finding nouns from verbs exercise, 74-77
See also finding nouns from verbs exercise prompts
finding nouns from verbs exercise prompts
___ flushes, 74-75
___ indicts, 75
___ operates, 76
___ paddles, 75-76
___ soars, 77
finding verbs from nouns exercise, 70-74
See also finding verbs from nouns exercise prompts
finding verbs from nouns exercise prompts
crossbow ___, 71
graduation ___, 73
kettle ___, 71-72
summer ___, 72-73
waitress ___, 72
first-person narrative, 28, 29, 44, 46, 115, 156, 201
Four Quartets, The, 1
free association, sense-bound, 8-9, 12, 18
fundamental tone, 88, 172
Giles, Rob, 110, 204, 218, 221
Gladwell, Malcolm, 24
Gora, Joy, 15, 25-26, 36, 37, 42, 218, 223
Greene, Emily, 218
group writing, 9-10, 47-48, 168
Halvorsen, Ann, 54, 56-57, 64, 73, 76, 79, 80, 81, 218
Harvey, Caroline, 85-86, 91-92, 136-137, 145, 155-156, 218, 220
Hayes, Bonnie, 58, 61, 71, 72, 75, 77, 82, 84, 218, 220
Henchy, Ian, 55, 57, 218
"I Can't Make You Love Me," 4
"In Memoriam," 215
"In Memoriam" quatrain, 215
keys, 68, 88
See also playing in keys exercise
Keys, Scarlet, 12, 135-136, 139-140, 142-143, 156-157, 159-161, 176-177, 181, 197, 198, 218
"Leave My Like Alone," 100
legato, 169
Leigh, Joanna, 218
Lewis, Sylvie, 112, 218
Linda M, 18-19, 22, 32, 218
linking qualities, 106, 108, 123, 124, 128, 129, 131, 145, 146
See also finding linking qualities exercises; linking qualities to target ideas exercise; linking qualities to target ideas working both directions exercise
linking qualities to target ideas exercise, 107-122
See also linking qualities to target ideas exercise prompts
linking qualities to target ideas exercise prompts
deep-sea diver, 113-118
guitar solo, 118-122
snowstorm, 107-113
linking qualities to target ideas working both directions exercise, 123-143
See also linking qualities to target ideas working both directions exercise prompts
linking qualities to target ideas working both directions exercise prompts
broken glass, 128-133
cheating lover, 138-143
falling in love, 134-138
sleeping late, 122-128
Lyle, Kami, 218
masculine rhymes, 185, 187
Matt K, 42, 44, 218
McLeod, Clare, 165, 176, 218
McMorrow, Mo, 16, 26-27, 28, 102, 103, 218
Meider, Jess, 56, 61-62, 64, 69, 71, 81 82, 131-132, 148-149, 163-164, 187, 193, 218
melodic shapes, 169, 170, 200
Merenda, James, 67-68, 218
metaphor challenges, 2
See also specific writing challenges, exercises, and prompts
metaphors, 12, 15, 19, 46, 49-51, 56, 57, 60, 62, 68, 70, 71, 88-89, 98, 99, 100, 104, 114, 122, 125, 161, 176, 177, 179, 183, 186, 187, 189, 195, 199, 201, 204, 205, 209, 217, 218
expressed identity, 50-51
extended, 105, 106, 215
looking for, 7, 137, 139, 175, 177, 179, 184, 188, 192, 194, 196, 199, 203, 207, 210, 213
qualifying, 51
stacking, 134-135, 143
verbal, 51, 111, 112
versus simile, 98
See also specific writing challenges, exercises, and prompts
meter. *See* common meter; duplo meter; pentameter lines; rhythm patterns; tetrameter lines; trimeter lines; triple meter
Miller, Nick, 18, 19, 218
Mitchell, Kaz, 16, 17, 20-21, 24, 34, 39, 43, 45-46, 47, 218

Mount, Sarah, 166, 218
"My Girl," 4
Neilson, Tami, 111-112, 115, 176, 218
Nosko, Leora, 28, 218
noun-noun collisions exercise. *See* expressed identity exercises
noun-verb collisions exercise, 67-70
  See also noun-verb collisions exercise prompts
noun-verb collisions exercise prompts
  autumn remembers, 69
  carburetor sings, 68-69
  funeral exhales, 68
  handkerchief pleads, 70
  moonlight tumbles, 67-68
nouns, 50, 51, 52, 59, 67, 89, 91, 92, 93, 94, 95, 97, 106, 171
  nondiatonic, 60
  See also adjective-noun collisions exercise; finding adjectives from nouns exercise; finding nouns from adjectives exercise; finding nouns from verbs exercise; finding verbs from nouns exercise; noun-verb collisions exercise
O'Shaughnessy, John, 25, 219
object writing, 5, 9, 12, 23, 52, 53, 59, 63, 70, 105-107
  elevator prompt, 7-8
  See also object writing challenge; "what" writing exercise; "when" writing exercise; "where" writing exercise; "who" writing exercise
object writing challenge, 2, 4-10
  See also "what" writing exercise; "when" writing exercise; "where" writing exercise; "who" writing exercise
object writing with metaphor challenge. *See* linking qualities to target ideas exercise; linking qualities to target ideas working both directions exercise; finding linking qualities exercises
"Ode to the West Wind," 51
Olmsted, Rebecca, 218
participles, 65
past tense, 32, 33
Pattison, Pat, 11, 12, 100-101, 140, 146, 178-179, 180, 187, 188
Pence, Charlotte, 85, 219
pentameter lines, 169, 202, 206-212
  See also common meter couplets and pentameter lines exercise; tetrameter couplets and pentameter lines exercise
Penton, Paul, 9, 15, 25, 30, 31, 38, 44, 45, 46, 219
perfect rhyme, 185, 205
personification, 53, 56, 69, 73, 87, 179, 184, 215
pitches, 169, 170, 171
playing in keys exercise
  finding linking qualities, 93-98
  using linking qualities, 88-93
  See also playing in keys exercise prompts
playing in keys exercise prompts
  cathedral, 92-83
  handshake, 96-97
  maple tree, 94
  policeman, 89-92
  sunrise, 97-98
  tide, 88-89
  traffic, 94-95
point of view, 198
Pope, Alexander, 168
prepositional phrase, 76
prepositions, 70, 172, 173
present tense, 32, 33, 34, 44, 46
primary stress, 170, 171, 190
  in compound words, 172
  See also stressed syllables
productive ambiguity, 56
prompts, 2, 3, 10
  See also specific writing challenge prompts; "what" writing exercise prompts; "when" writing exercise prompts; "where" writing exercise prompts; "who" writing exercise prompts
pronouns, 75
  personal, 172
  relative, 172
Quilter, Deborah, 8, 24-25, 32, 33, 34, 38, 43, 44, 46, 219, 222
Rajwani, Tasleem, 29, 219
Rawlings, David, 168
Reid, Mike, 4
rhyme, 169, 217
  assonance, 190
  consonance, 196, 200, 205
  feminine, 185, 187
  masculine, 185, 187
  partial, 208
  perfect, 185, 205
  types, 183
rhyming positions, 204
rhythm, 169-175, 217
rhythm and rhyme writing challenges, 2-3
rhythm patterns, 173-175, 202
  duple, 173-174, 178, 181, 184, 186, 188
  triple, 174, 181, 184, 185, 186, 188
Robinson, Smokey, 4
Roget's International Thesaurus, 59

Romans, Ben, 53, 58, 219, 222
Salo, Leora, 67, 219
second-person narrative, 30, 44, 179, 184, 201
secondary stress, 170, 190, 194
in compound words, 172
in grammatical functions, 173
See also stressed syllables
Seiffert, Catrina, 27, 28, 35, 219
sense-bound writing, 2, 4-5, 9, 41, 47, 105, 110, 112, 113, 115, 116, 117, 119, 121, 175, 176, 179, 184, 186, 188, 189, 192, 194, 196, 199, 203, 204, 207, 208, 210, 211, 213
See also free association, sense-bound
senses, 5-6
See also sense-bound writing; free association, sense-bound
Shamblin, Alan, 4
Shelley, Percy Bysshe, 51
Shorr, Michael, 110-111, 219
simile exercise, 102-103
See also simile exercise prompts
simile exercise prompts
a bad joke is like, 102
divorce is like, 102-103
hope is like, 103
trust is like, 102
a waterfall is like, 103
similes, 12, 15, 46, 83, 98-104, 111, 114, 128, 131, 151, 155-156, 157, 160, 162, 183, 186, 187, 189, 204, 209
versus metaphor, 98
See also simile exercise
Simon, Paul, 174
songwriters. *See names of specific songwriters*
Speace, Amy, 219
"Still Crazy After All These Years," 174
Sting, 23, 175
"Stolen Car," 23, 175
Stolpe, Andrea, 59, 60, 64-65, 66, 68, 70, 80, 82-83, 94, 96, 102, 103, 192-193, 194, 198, 199, 208, 219
stressed syllables, 168, 169, 170, 171, 172, 173, 200, 208
in compound words, 172
See also primary stress; secondary stress
Stübinger, Manuel, 28-29, 34, 219
Swiniarski, Stan, 141, 144, 193-194, 199-200, 208, 210, 211, 219
target idea, 106, 108, 123, 124, 129, 131, 144, 146
See also specific writing challenges, exercises, and prompts; linking qualities to target ideas exercise; linking qualities to target ideas working both directions exercise
Tennyson, Alfred Lord, 215
tetrameter couplets, 168, 169, 192, 201, 202
See also tetrameter couplets and pentameter lines exercise; tetrameter couplets exercise
tetrameter couplets and pentameter lines exercise, 201-205
See also tetrameter couplets and pentameter lines exercise prompts
tetrameter couplets and pentameter lines exercise prompts
war zone, 203-204
wildflowers, 205
tetrameter couplets exercise, 179-190
See also tetrameter couplets exercise prompts
tetrameter couplets exercise prompts
avalanche, 180-182
broken glass, 187-188
John Brown, 186-187
mountain, 182-183
rocking chair on the front porch at sunset, 189-190
skydiving, 188-189
sleeping late, 185-186
snowstorm, 183-184
train, 184-185
tetrameter lines, 174, 175, 181, 184, 186, 187, 190, 197, 199, 202, 206, 209, 213, 215
See also tetrameter lines exercise
tetrameter lines exercise, 175-179
See also tetrameter lines exercise prompts
tetrameter lines exercise prompts
art museum, 176-177
digging for gold, 177-178
pickup truck, 178-179
sunset, 175-176
third-person narrative, 29, 30
timed writing, 6-7
To, Shirley, 21, 219
"Tomorrow We'll See," 23
tone center, 49
Tozier, Nicholas, 40, 219
trimeter lines, 175, 190-191, 192, 194, 197, 199, 209, 213, 215
triple meter, 169, 183, 193
unstable (abba) structure exercise, 212-216
See also unstable (abba) structure exercise prompts
unstable (abba) structure exercise

prompts
cloudy day, 214-215
sleeping late, 215-216
unstressed syllables, 169, 170, 171, 172, 173, 200, 208
verbs, 20, 50, 51, 54, 59, 65, 67, 89, 91, 92, 93, 94, 95, 97, 106, 171
active, 68
auxiliary, 172
choice, 188
giving commands with, 198
ing form, 33
intransitive, 70, 76, 77
metaphor-based, 19
strong, 19
tense-neutral, 33, 34
transitive, 75, 77
See also finding nouns from verbs exercise; finding verbs from nouns exercise; noun-verb collisions exercise
voice, writing, 2
Ward, Tanja, 24, 28, 219
Welch, Gillian, 17, 19, 168, 180, 182, 184, 185, 186-187, 217, 219
"what" writing exercise, 10-23, 31
See also "what" writing exercise prompts
"what" writing exercise prompts
arrow, 22-23
bathroom mirror, 13-14
bouquet, 19-20
cigar, 21-22
crash, 11-12
curb, 18-19
dentist, 14-15
feather, 17-18
hair, 17
lily pad, 12-13
movie theater, 20-21
rain cloud, 20
screwdriver, 15
sky, 10-11
umbrella, 16
"when" writing exercise, 10, 31-39
seasonal, 31, 35
special occasion, 31
time of day, 31, 35
See also "when" writing exercise prompts
"when" writing exercise prompts
crossing the finish line, 39
Easter Sunday, 36-37
first snowfall, 36
graduation, 33-34
late evening, 37-38
loved one's funeral, 38
six in the morning, 35
summer rainstorm, 32-33
wedding rehearsal dinner, 34
"where" writing exercise, 10, 39-47
See also "where" writing exercise prompts
"where" writing exercise prompts
canoe on the river, 47
cliff by the ocean, 40
hotel bar, 42
old fishing hole, 43-44
on the city bus, 45-46
park bench in the city, 40-42
suburban swimming pool, 42-43
under an umbrella, 44-45
wedding in an old church, 46-47
"who" writing exercise, 10, 23-31, 62
character development and, 23
See also "who" writing exercise prompts
"who" writing exercise prompts
ballerina, 29-30
balloon man, 26-27
cyclist, 38-29
homeless child, 27-28
priest, 25-26
puppy, 30-31
sailor, 24
trucker, 28
waitress clearing table, 24-25
Wilkinson, Scott, 26, 219
Worsham, Charlie, 90-91, 97, 102, 113, 115-116, 119, 120-121, 125-126, 129-130, 132-133, 219
Wright, Richard, 105
Writing Better Lyrics, 9, 34, 88, 179, 190, 198, 209
writing challenges. *See specific writing challenges, exercises, and prompts*
writing exercises. *See specific writing challenges, exercises, and prompts*